Resurrection

Pat Howorth
P.O. Box 1428
Slidell, LA 70459
1-504-641-0093

RESURRECTION
Release From Oppression

Morton Kelsey

**With an Epilogue by
Howard L. Rice**

PAULIST PRESS
New York ◆ Mahwah

For my grandson
Weston Seth Kelsey,
to share with him
the mystery of the resurrection

The Publisher gratefully acknowledges the use of the following materials: excerpts from *The Man Born to Be King* by Dorothy L. Sayers, published by Victor Gollancz Ltd, London, used by permission of David Higham Associates Limited, London; two stanzas of Howard Chandler Robbins' hymn, "And Have the Bright Immensities," published in *The Hymnal of the Episcopal Church in the U.S.A.*, reprinted by permission of Morehouse Barlow Co., Inc.

Cover art, "The Mystery of Faith" by Ben Long IV, is taken from a mural on display at St. Mary's Episcopal Church, West Jefferson, N.C. Used by permission.

Library of Congress
Catalog Card Number: 84-62150

ISBN: 0-8091-2673-7

Published by Paulist Press
997 Macarthur Boulevard
Mahwah, New Jersey 07430

Printed and bound in the
United States of America

CONTENTS

When some beloved voice that was to you
Both sound and sweetness, faileth suddenly,
And silence against which you dare not cry,
Aches round you like a strong disease and new—
What hope? what help? what music will undo
That silence to your sense? Not friendship's sigh—
Not reason's subtle count. Not melody
Of Viols, nor of pipes that Faunus blew—
Not songs of poets, nor of nightingales,
Whose hearts leap upward through the cypress trees
To the clear moon; nor yet the spheric laws
Self-chanted,—nor the angels' sweet "All hails,"
Met in the smile of God. Nay, none of these.
Speak *Thou*, availing Christ!—and fill this pause.

Elizabeth Barrett Browning
"Substitution"

Introduction

Writing about the resurrection of Jesus of Nazareth is a difficult and awesome task. Jesus' rising from the dead confronts us with the center and heart of the Christian faith, the very soul of Christianity. The historical resurrection and its transforming power remade Jesus' broken band of disciples and sent them forth victoriously into a hostile and persecuting empire. Because of their resurrection faith many of them risked and lost their lives. The resurrection made it worth it.

The message of the early Church centered on this momentous event; preaching the resurrection of Jesus caught the imagination of the jaded ancient world and gave it new vitality. The emphasis on Jesus' rising from the dead in the reign of Tiberius Caesar clearly distinguished Christianity from the other faiths that were contending for the allegiance of the many different peoples who were part of the Roman Empire. Today belief in the resurrection is one of the main tenets of Christianity that separates it from other world religions.

Informed Christians know every Sunday is a little Easter. Christians come together on the first day of the week (not the sabbath) to rejoice and celebrate because it was on this day of the week that Jesus rose from the dead. The central act of Christian worship on this day is the celebration of the Eucharist, Holy Communion or Mass. This service reenacts Jesus' crucifixion on Golgotha and his death-destroying resurrection three days later. The various names for the service simply point to different aspects of Jesus' incredible victory over evil and death.

For forty years the resurrection of Jesus has been the keystone of my life and belief. Over the years I had studied and written about different parts of the narrative devoted to Jesus' rising from the dead. When I started to work on the general theme of this event of history, I realized that I had never tried to fit the different accounts together. The cockier biblical criticism current when I was in seminary forty years ago had discouraged me from looking for a consecutive narrative. To my delight and surprise I found that as I studied and meditated over the texts of Paul and the four Gospels a continuous, powerful and remarkably consistent account emerged before me. There were far fewer inconsistencies and contradictions in the various accounts of this event than I had been led to believe. The whole narrative made a fresh, new impact on me.

In the following pages I present a picture of what happened on Easter Sunday and on the days following Easter as the risen Jesus met with his disciples and friends. I have remained close to the Greek texts and yet bring these various accounts of the resurrection into a harmonious story. I have used my imagination to explore in depth these events that are often described tersely and to elaborate elements in a way that, I hope, is not inconsistent with the original. I have also provided a psychological understanding of the chief characters who witnessed these events.

Gerald O'Collins has written a survey of recent theories about the resurrection entitled *What Are They Saying About the Resurrection?* In it he notes that the well-known American author Amos Wilder has written: "Imagination is a necessary component of all profound knowing and celebration. . . . It is at the level of imagination that any full engagement with life takes place." O'Collins then goes on to observe: "It could well be that the lack of images to shape and motivate contemplation of the resurrection has stopped many from celebrating that mystery profoundly in their prayer and becoming fully engaged with it."[1] I have tried to provide some valid images that can help people engage with resurrection as readily and fully as they do with Jesus' betrayal and crucifixion.

I also discuss why the story as I present it is one that reasonable people of our modern day can accept as historical. Most of the reasons offered for rejecting the resurrection narrative are inadequate when carefully examined. We live in a much more open

universe than the one envisioned by those who lived at the beginning of our century. The more we allow ourselves to be engaged
with the person of the risen Jesus, the more plausible the whole
story becomes.

I have interspersed the narrative with reflections and reactions to the events as they took place. I considered placing these
reflections at the end of the story; however, we can understand
the latter parts of the narrative better if we reflect imaginatively
upon each event as it occurred.

As I went further and further into the accounts of Jesus' rising, I found that it was impossible to understand the full meaning
of the resurrection without looking at the life of Jesus which pre-
ceded this event and the reactions of his disciples which followed
it. The resurrection is part of a larger picture of God coming into
the world to redeem it. God in Jesus came into the world as an infant born of a woman. Jesus lived the full human and divine life,
died on the cross and rose again. God then poured out the spirit
of Jesus, the Holy Spirit, upon those who would accept it. The
resurrection is the central act of the drama of God reaching out to
human beings to bring them to their highest destiny.

The Western world of which we are part was traditionally
Christian but has been taken over by secular and materialistic
thinking. It is nearly impossible for us to live both in the resurrection world view and in the basic framework of rationalistic
materialism at the same time. Most of us raised in Western culture have been tainted by its skepticism toward spiritual things
and particularly by the possibility of the spiritual affecting the
physical world. I found it refreshing recently to hear Bishop Peter Kwong reminding his largely Chinese clergy in Hong Kong
that real Christianity always has two dimensions, the transcen-
dental and the this-worldly. The crucifixion-resurrection is the
most extreme example of the influence of the spiritual within and
upon the materialistic world. The victory of Easter is the proclamation that the God of love has final dominion over every aspect of this universe in which we live.

As children of our age, we face this statement confronted
with our own deep doubts. But honest doubt and questioning can
lead us further into conviction and commitment if we engage
them seriously. George Buttrick wrote in his commentary in *The*

Interpreter's Bible: "Doubt is perhaps not the opposite of faith, but only faith's misgivings. We could hardly doubt what does not exist; if we doubt God, we have perhaps therefore already glimpsed him. We need not fear doubt unless it comes from sin; there is faith in honest doubt." He quotes Philip Bailey's poem "Festus: A Country Town":

> Who never doubted never half believed.
> Where doubt there truth is—'tis his shadow.

He concludes that the "opposite of faith is not doubt, but cynicism."[2] The best antidote for doubt is more experience of the continuing power of the risen Jesus in our lives.

When I began to understand the resurrection narrative and what it did for the early Christians, it forced me to look at my own Christian commitment and compare it with theirs. That examination was humiliating and brought me back to the risen Jesus, asking forgiveness and greater strength and courage. Also, as we try to participate in this central Christian mystery and then share it with others, we attack the fortress of evil itself. That evil and darkness should counterattack is not surprising to those who have known the powers of darkness. When we ask for the help of the Christ to repulse that attack, we again know the power and victory of the resurrected Jesus.

I am deeply grateful to many people who helped me establish, confirm and strengthen my resurrection faith. For many years the congregation at St. Luke's Church, Monrovia, California, responded to my attempts to express the centrality of Easter. The students at the University of Notre Dame were eager for solid affirmation of that conviction. John Sanford and I have talked over this aspect of our faith many times and I have read with profit the expositions of the resurrection contained in his privately printed sermons. Dr. Andrew Canale has found the resurrection of Jesus and his continuing risen presence as important as I in his personal and professional journey and has recently published an excellent book, *Understanding the Human Jesus*, dealing with his humanity and resurrection. We have shared our experiences of healing encounters with this presence. The commentaries in *The Interpreter's Bible* have been an invaluable aid, as have the books of Raymond Brown, particularly his two-volume commentary, *The Gospel According to John*. Long a fan of Dorothy Sayers, I found her radio plays on the life of Jesus, *The Man Born To Be King*, profoundly moving, convincing and powerful. Her final play on the resurrection opened my eyes to the possibility of writing a consecutive narrative of this event. My friend John Whalen has edited the manuscript and has been a companion on the inner journey with the risen Christ. Another friend, Maury Amen, helped me put the final manuscript together. Cindy Wesley transformed my terrible typescript into readable condition. Joanne Brooks has helped reading proofs. I am grateful to Don Brophy, my editor at Paulist Press, who was interested in this project and allowed me the time so that the material could develop at its own pace. My wife, Barbara, has worked through this entire manuscript with me. We have shared our hopes in the resurrection for forty years. My friend, Howard Rice, consented to add a final chapter on resurrection and social justice and I thank him for adding this dimension to the book.

I do not capitalize pronouns that refer to Jesus, since it would make the text look stilted. We need to remember that Jesus was divine and *human*. The biblical quotations are in most instances translated by me from the Greek text.

Gualala, California
Easter 1984

1.

A Way of Hope

For many months something deep within me has been prompting me to write about the resurrection of Jesus. I was asked to speak at Eastertime and I looked over some talks that I had given on the resurrection throughout the years. I realized that very little has been written in recent years on the subject of the resurrection of Jesus of Nazareth and its very crucial place in Christian life and thought. I had written about the cross and its meaning, but not at length on the resurrection. Through a very busy schedule my mind and heart turned back again and again to this event. I realized that this was something that I could not deal with until I was free of other things and was quiet and open to the subject.

Finally such a time occurred in my life. I had put aside my busyness and spent a month in reflection on the meaning of the Church and Christianity. But when I started to write nothing came. Everything I put down seemed wrong. None of the ideas seemed to jell. I made three or four starts which led nowhere. One night I awoke and was meditating before the Christ. First of all I realized that I was blocked. The darkness rather than the light seemed to hover near me and I asked Christ, the faithful inner companion, what was blocking me. The inner voice replied that I had to listen to what the darkness was saying and then went on to say: "I cannot help you with what you do not face. I cannot save you from a situation that you will not admit."

I had heard this message many times before, but it is so easy to forget this inner voice and get caught in busyness and egotism and worldly concerns. Spiritual growth is a continual process and for some a constant battle against the forces that would keep us from our spiritual destiny. Scupoli's book, *The Spiritual Combat*, had brought that home to me many years before. It is very hard to listen to the darkness without being overwhelmed with it. The darkness knows all of our faults and presses them home against us and then builds them into hopeless obstacles. In spite of this I listened and I heard the darkness speaking.

Dark Voice (in a sneering tone)—At last you listen to me. It is time. You can't write anything significant on this subject. You know perfectly well that there is no reality to resurrection, that it is false. In addition you can't write. This is one you can't pull off. Besides, you are such a hopeless slob, depraved and vile, caught in the commercialism and passions of this world. If there were any risen Christ (which of course there isn't) he wouldn't want anything to do with you, you wretched, deceived and miserable mess. I am the only reality. You are in my power and sooner or later you will have to acknowledge me and join me. Behind you and around you are my minions. You are my prisoner.

(I am aware of those minions as dark shadows. I feel their slimy, foul hands seize me and feel their blows and their kicks, and so I call out again to the risen Lord for help as I have so many times before.)

Me—Lord, this is why I fear listening to the darkness. I am surrounded and bound, attacked, beaten. Lord, come and deliver me. For this reason you came and defeated evil on the cross. Lord, help me escape from the inner destroyer and its power.

Dark Voice—Call all you want, you worthless fraud, deceiver and deceived. You are in my power. You belong to me.

(The blows of the minions continue to rain down on me. They throw filth and offal at me. Gradually their attack ceases, and even though my eyes are closed I feel a presence. There is a light which warms my body and even penetrates through my closed eyes. I no longer feel their awful hands upon me; the blows and kicks cease. I open my eyes. A magnificent light fills the dark and ugly cavern where I stand. My adversaries have fallen back and are seeking cracks and crevices in the rock in which to hide. The light continues to increase until I shut my eyes. The ropes and shackles fall from my hands and legs. I open my eyes and there before me as if congealed

out of the light stands the risen One with arms outstretched toward me. Even though I am free physically I seem unable to move. How can I reach out to such purity and holiness? He steps up to me and embraces me, filth and all. Like the prodigal I bury my head in his bosom and weep. Finally I am able to speak.)

Me—Thank you, my Lord, thank you. I did not realize that I was in their power until I stopped and listened to the darkness, until I faced that negative ugly presence. But how can you embrace one such as I?

Inner Voice—I love you and all humankind. Your dirt does not bother me; my light cannot be sullied by it. I am with you humans always. I was waiting for your call. I do not force myself upon you. Thank you for calling and allowing me to come.

Me—Lord, what happened? How did I fall into the darkness again?

Inner Voice—The whys are not that important. Freedom is the important matter, but you do need to know. A part of you is quite contaminated by the darkness, and when you are not very conscious it drags the rest of you down into the darkness even when you are not aware of it.

Me—Thank you, Lord, for your power over darkness and for your resurrection, for your love which knows the pain and reality of human evil and came to free us from them, the love of your cross and resurrection which defeated the evil one.

Inner Voice—Let us now go where you can be washed clean and start again. Let us get out of this dark and ugly place.

He takes me by the hand and leads me over the uneven floor up toward a black crack in the jagged wall. He leads me through this entrance to a tunnel. It slopes gradually upward and in no time I see another kind of light, natural light, and soon we emerge into the daylight in the secret garden to which I have been brought many times before. The great spring of warm water breaks forth from the cliff and falls into a clear and bub-

bling pool. We both swim in the pool and I can feel both my outer and inner beings cleansed. Then we climb back onto the meadow, and there I fall asleep in the warm sun, lying close to the saving One.

When I awake the sun is setting and he tells me it is time to go on. We walk down along the stream which flows from the pool to the ocean. Standing in the surf we watch the sun turn the sky into a symphony of colors. We ascend the stone steps up to the sun-warmed cabin perched high on the cliff. We enter, and he makes a fire upon the great hearth and then sets a simple meal before us and we eat. Before long I am drowsy, and he takes me to my bunk where I sleep, listening to the wind through the trees and feeling confident in the presence near me.

(After this meditation I returned to bed to rest and sleep. In the morning I got up and after breakfast I went to the typewriter. Usually I dialogue with the Inner Voice in my written journal, but this time I wanted to be able to follow the images and ideas as they came, and so I used the typewriter to focus my attention and bring me before Christ's presence. I began to write.)

Me—Lord, I need your help if anything that I have to say has any real value. I want to write what you wish. I think that something needs to be written and that I have something to say, but it is not coming together. I have many different motives for writing, but the best part of me wants to share how you have rescued me again and again and helped me to work toward wholeness. I am refreshed and ready to go. Please help me. Where are you?

Inner voice—Here within you and around you.

Me—In my immaturity I need you more concretely.

Inner Voice—Return to where you were last night with me.

(I return in imagination to the cabin and I see its interior, the great hearth and the fire blazing on it, the sun rising over the forest, and then I feel a tap on my shoulder. It is my Lord. I turn and he embraces me. Light shines from the wound scars in his hands and feet. These are brighter than the light which surrounds him, and that is brighter than the sunrise. My mind and heart are cleared; joy and peace and a sense of wholeness well up within me. We sit down at the polished wooden table and he speaks:)

Inner Voice—What can I do for you?

Me—You are my life, my light and my salvation, my hope, my meaning, my only saving help when the forces of darkness attack me and try to drag me off to hell. I know that I am in the world and very much of the world, and I know that this world passes and disappears and that only you and Abba-Father's Kingdom give final meaning and substance to us human beings. I want this writing to make the resurrection more real to me, and to share with others that you have conquered evil and that there is hope no matter how black things look in the outer world or in our hearts. You can and will save us again and again and again from our folly, dishonesty, and destructiveness and even from death itself. How do I get this message across?

Inner Voice—What is it that you really want to say?

Me—I want to share that by your life and resurrection and risen presence you bring us through the dark places of life to an eternal victory.

Inner Voice—Tell your own story first. Share how and why I have become so central to you. Don't worry about logic and order. When you have finished your story then you can try to understand it and explain it to yourself and to others like you.
   (I began to write and my own very personal story emerged. I saw that there was no way to speak of resurrection except to give a concrete example of how it still saves us.)

A Personal Story

   The resurrection of Jesus from the dead gives me hope. It is the only event in history in which I have seen evil and ugliness, pain and violence, destructiveness and death confronted, defeated, transcended and transmuted. The evil of this world is very real to me. I have experienced a lot of pain and destructiveness within me and around me. Much of my life has been hard and full of tension. The resurrection makes it worth the struggle.

I doubt very much that I could muster much realistic hope if Jesus had not risen. If he had gone up to Golgotha, to the place of the skull, and died nobly and that was the end of it, I would admire him as an heroic human being, but human existence would look like a trivial, meaningless farce. If love and glory were not somehow manifested *in this world*, I would doubt their ultimate reality and power. I *know* the power of evil and destructiveness, attacking us within in depression and despair and outwardly in war and poverty. I know the law of the jungle that the strong feed on the weak. I know that death lies ahead for all of us whether in nuclear holocaust or by sudden death or by a lingering painful death. If these for us are not somewhere defeated in history, is there any ultimate meaning or hope?

Many times I have waited by the bedside of dying people—a teenager with sarcoma, a young adult with melanoma, a young mother whose children needed her, middle-aged people afraid of the loneliness of death, the aged who feared that there was nothing before them. But it was the death of my mother when I was twenty-one that made the greatest impact. This event was critical for me. She was the kindest and most gentle and loving person that I had known. She had her problems, like the rest of us, and they left their imprint too, but love covers a multitude of sins and love was there. I sat by her and watched that love and concern crushed and broken over many months and then snuffed out.

And then the darkness descended. The feeble beliefs I had been given in Sunday school and church evaporated. They were largely given to me by people who did not know what they believed. One or two of the friends of my family had been touched deeply by the reality of love, but in the company town where I was reared they were considered unrealistic and were mocked behind their backs. I truly doubted that there was any substance to belief in God and love or goodness and kindness. The best person I knew had been destroyed by illness, and I remember how often her belief in God and love had been the butt of jokes and ridicule in our "realistic" household. The darkness descended and I was in pain, searing pain. I had just finished college and I went on to study philosophy at Princeton Graduate School. There I found that Christianity was the butt of jokes too. I remember one particular occasion when the head of the department was leading a seminar on Plato. I made some comment on the relevance of Christianity to the subject and the professor said in derision: "Ha, Kelsey is a Christian and he will enlighten us." At the same time I read Immanuel Kant's *Critique of Pure Reason* with an excellent tutor. We worked at it until I understood it. It was one of the most creative and most devastating experiences of my life. It taught me to think and it also swept away every shred of my poorly understood belief. My belief system collapsed—all of it.

The trouble with most agnostics is that they are not agnostic enough. They hold on to what they want to believe and they toss aside what they find difficult and inconvenient. Real agnosticism takes away beliefs in God, meaning, morals, everything. I was left in a stormy sea with a gale raging and no anchor. With no guidelines left I tried paths most people would not consider. When I later read *The Confessions* I could understand Augustine's experience in decadent Rome. It is still painful to look back on that period of my life.

As I reflected on my youth I saw that it had contained little joy except for the one bright candle of love and meaning shining through my mother (and this had been snuffed out). Born a blue baby in a little midwestern town and kept warm in a shoebox by the woodstove, I struggled from the beginning to stay alive. My head had been crushed at birth and this resulted in hearing problems and emotional liability. My family feared that I was mentally defective. Some of the relatives wrote to each other that it was a great pity that such a child had been given to such fine parents, and I am sure that at times my father and mother felt the same way. They even considered sending me to a home for retarded children. An IQ test saved me. I have great appreciation for those who created the Stanford-Binet. They gave it to me in third grade, and they were so surprised at the results that they gave it to me again. It became clear that mental deficiency was not my problem.

Childhood was one sickness after another—infections in the winter and allergies in the summer. I could walk by poison ivy and come down with it. It was a struggle to stay alive and compete. I never could do what the others did in athletics, and, as I have said elsewhere, I had the coordination of a palsied hippopotamus. When I told my childhood story to an analyst in Zurich she remarked: "Your family gave you just enough love to keep you alive."

I left graduate school at twenty-two. I found a job teaching junior high children in a Peekskill military school, just to make a living, with the stormy sea raging all around me, the blackness like a pack of vicious dogs nipping at me from every direction. An additional irony was that I was given a school football team to coach! I remember walking around a frozen lake in January supervising the youngsters as they skated and wondering if I could ever find any meaning. It looked like a truly meaningless and friendless world. Near Peekskill was a small Episcopal church where I went for several Sundays and was warmly received. The minister was actually rather intelligent. It gave me an idea. I would try the church to see if Christianity really had any meaning. I had thought of other things to do, but I knew they wouldn't have any answers to my deepest doubts, my fears that life was all a big, bad joke.

Off I went to seminary with no other conviction than that I might find some meaning there in the training ground for Christianity. My father knew the bishop and that was a help in being accepted. In those days there was a lack of ministerial students. Pearl Harbor was bombed during my first semester. One seminary turned me down and I certainly don't blame the staff from one point of view, as my reasons for coming were unusual. Another saw that my academic record was impeccable and accepted me. The professors fed my intellect. Unlike many of the students, I had no problems with biblical criticism or the questioning of orthodox belief by the teachers. Anything that they could give me was something that filled the great agnostic void. The teachers were as intelligent as those who had made fun of Christianity at Princeton, and I found and read Baron von Hügel and A.E. Taylor, two thinkers far more intelligent than the professors at graduate school, philosophers who stacked up to Kant and Plato, Schopenhauer and Aristotle. Von Hügel and Taylor were convinced Christians. Von Hügel himself had been rescued out of a darkness like mine by Abbé Huvelin, the great French spiritual director.

I began to see that the cross and resurrection were the center of Christianity. There was little doubt that Jesus of Nazareth had been crucified. The historical evidence for this was as good as the evidence for the reality of Julius Caesar. And if he did indeed rise again, then the best of human beings (who knew all the worst that humankind and the dull meaningless world could do) had not been snuffed out. It was as if at last I could see the hand and power of God written in the fabric of human history. Here was some real evidence.

Even though in seminary I began to get the right intellectual answers, somehow I did not know how to integrate them into my life. I was still plagued with anxiety. I saw no hope for meaning in this war-torn world without the resurrection. However, I did not know how to bring this meaning into the center of my being. I believed intellectually that Jesus was indeed raised from the dead in Palestine some nineteen hundred years ago, but this wasn't enough to banish all of my pain and fears and doubts. I tried everything that anyone suggested seriously.

In seminary I found that a group of students were already in the chapel when I arrived for the daily chapel service. I was curious and came earlier and earlier and discovered that eight to ten students came every morning for a half hour of private quiet time for meditation, prayer and reading. They read classics of Christian devotion like *The Imitation of Christ*, William Law's *Serious Call to a Devout and Holy Life* and *The Confessions* of Augustine. This group prayer provided some help, but I later found that the administration considered this group far too emotionally involved and suspected them of imbalance. When I became a minister and got into the parish environment I did not have a similar group of silent companions, and so even this practice fell away until I heard Charles Whiston, an Episcopal priest who had written a book on the devotional life, speak about the life of prayer. Then I began to use morning and evening prayer daily and to keep a list of people whom I brought before God.

During my ministry at Immanuel Church I met and was married to my wife, Barbara. She has been my companion for over forty years; we have three children and four grandchildren. When we are struggling for meaning, struggling to find our place in the total scheme of things, it is essential that we have support in "this world." My experience was similar to Jung's, who wrote: "My family and my profession remained the base to which I would always return, assuring me that I was an actual existing, ordinary person."¹ The love, understanding and support I have received from my family members have helped me to work through the doubts and darkness which often attacked me. My professional life also gave me a base from which to work on integrating my life and belief.

I left my first mission and went to Phoenix where I was assistant to the dean of the cathedral. The dean gave me great freedom and I started a healing service following one of the eucharistic celebrations. I regret to say that the motivation for starting it was more to compete with churches that had such services than burning conviction. But a few healings began to occur and a group of people coming to these services wanted to stay and pray together. We brought Charles Whiston to the cathedral, and then I was introduced to the well-known healer, Agnes Sanford, and saw with my own eyes that the power of God could move through human beings today in the same way as recorded in the Acts of the Apostles and in the Gospels.

I was called to a parish in California, and there I tried to make the greatest impact that a minister could make, again for the wrong reasons. And again the darkness and anxiety struck me down. Something was missing. I could find no Christian minister to help me in this time of despair, but a Quaker friend, Dorothy Phillips, listened to me and suggested that I see a Jungian analyst, Max Zeller. With two others Dorothy had written a book entitled *The Choice Is Always Ours* which showed that depth psychology spoke of the same realities as the devotional masters of all ages. The Church had forgotten how to use the methods that enabled people to tap the reality of the spiritual world.

How interesting to learn about Christianity from a Jew who had escaped a concentration camp in Nazi Germany by a series of quite astounding circumstances. I will never forget him telling me how after this experience he never doubted God's reality and power. With him and two other analysts, Hilde and James Kirsch, I came to see why I had not been able to live my life without overwhelming anxiety. They shared with me what they had learned from Dr. C. G. Jung about ways of dealing with the depth and agony of the human soul. Through Jung and these followers of his I began to perceive three reasons why I had not been able to integrate the resurrection into the core of my being.

These three realizations provided a method for connecting with this reality. First, as I listened to my dreams I discovered that a wisdom greater than my own, the very providence of God, was trying to get my attention and lead me out of the morass in which I was sinking. This led to a second realization. In the depth of the night when I got up angry because I could not sleep, I found that the same Love was there seeking my fellowship. With this presence I could talk about any subject—my doubts, my failures, my mistakes, my sins, my fears, my questions. This presence spoke with the same power and wisdom evidenced in the historical Jesus of Nazareth and with the same love and insight that praying people claimed they found as they came in touch with the risen Jesus, the Lord Christ.

Third, I realized that one of the reasons I was anxious was that I was split in two. My intellect and my worldly side had been taught that only this physical world was real. One part of me accepted unquestioningly the materialistic thesis that there is no meaning in the universe, that this physical world evolved out of blind, meaningless chaos, that human beings are only the materialistic gene's way of reproducing itself. On the other side was my experience with spiritual reality, my actual experience of providence, grace and love, which had reduced my anxiety. Until this split could be healed I would be torn apart inside; in fact, that feeling of being torn apart is exactly what much of my anxiety was. The resurrection confronted me with my inner split and gave me a way to heal it.

My anxiety and depression were abscesses on my soul which needed to be lanced. Until I dealt with their pain I could not be healed. I could not bring about their healing until I began to realize that we human beings share in both a real physical world and a real spiritual dimension and that these have a profound influence on each other. What I do in my prayer and meditation has a profound effect upon my body and actions. What I do with my life in work and play and how I relate to other human beings has an impact upon my relationship with the spiritual world.

This intellectual framework which von Hügel and A. E.

Taylor had provided was now filled out and completed by my own experience. The steel framework of the skyscraper was filled with enclosing walls, with floors, with elevators and separate rooms. I had been given a way of allowing the risen Christ to meet me and touch every aspect of my life and my anxieties began to dissipate.

Through Jung and his followers I was given a new map of reality. On this map the resurrection became for me the central event. The life and death of Jesus, his birth and ascension and the coming of the Spirit were all part of the Christian drama of which the resurrection was the central act, the keystone that holds together the whole arch of vital Christianity. Without the resurrection there might be a spiritual world and a life after death, but they might also be no better than this world in which we live with its poverty, racial hatred, power-driven egotism, misery, war, brutality, systematized torture (of which the cross is one of the more hideous examples), pain, agony and despair. A spiritual dimension without the resurrection might well be far worse than extinction.

Along with these things I learned about the reality of evil and the evil one, and was given a way to deal with the source of evil in the world and in myself. I found that there was no evil within me that could withstand the presence of the risen One. For much of my life I had been engulfed from time to time with periods of depression and anxiety where hope was extinguished and I was literally battered by the dark destructiveness of evil. It is true that malfunctioning of the brain and of the intricate physical bodily systems can cause depression, but it is also true that some depression can result from bereavement, meaninglessness, hopelessness. As we confront the tragedies of misfortune, sickness, war, betrayal, unfaced anger and extinction in death we may trigger a physical mechanism that results in overwhelming depression.

As William James pointed out, if we are indeed part and parcel of a meaningless universe, the kind in which Jesus could be murdered on a cross with no resurrection, then being depressed only makes good sense. Under these conditions the sensitive and sensible person will be depressed. I have discovered only one event in history that redeemed all this evil for me and gave me hope: the resurrection of Jesus. Allowing the resurrected One to be constantly present, I can deal with all the evil suffered by Jesus, by my friends, and by me. I can face all the rape, pillage, war and hatred that I hear about daily, and still have hope. The resurrection reveals the ultimate nature of the universe, and the risen Christ continues to give victory over the power of evil.

There is still another kind of depression that does not seem to be triggered by any known outer pain or crisis. Sometimes it is as if the darkness seizes me and I have no power of my own to tear myself away from it. Sometimes I feel as though I have fallen into the pit of hell and demons of hell are using their most exquisite tortures to force me to give myself up to them. Many of us seem to live on the edge of the abyss and the cliffs are constantly crumbling away even when our outer life tells us that we should feel fine. I have discovered that those souls which, like mine, have been worn thin by misery and lack of love as children are open to the direct intrusion of that destructive, down-pulling, befouling spirit which has caused so much misery in our broken and suffering world.

These inner experiences of evil can often trigger the physical symptoms of depression as completely as brain disease, hormonal imbalance or outer tragedy. I believe that this destructive reality is one factor in most kinds of depression. The good news is that we are given a particular way to be released from this kind of inner agony. When I engage my depression rather than trying to run away from it, allow it to be expressed in imaginative pictures or images, and then ask the risen Christ to enter and free me from my inner tormentors, usually I am soon free of the depression. The gruesome darkness retreats and I am accepted and loved by the Christ. Many friends who are attacked in the same way have been lifted out of the pit by this method and enabled to go about the business of life again.

I began this chapter with one example of this method. I have described this practice in detail in several of my books.[2] The power of the imagination in opening us up to reality is far greater than most of us realize. Einstein's statement on the subject of imagination is comforting: "When I examine myself and my methods of thought I come to the conclusion that the gift of fantasy has meant more to me than my talent for abstract, positive thinking."[3]

The gift that opened Einstein to the structure and reality of the physical world can open us even more certainly to the depth of the spiritual world. As I have returned again and again and again through imagination to the resurrection and the resurrected One, this event has filled one part of my soul after another and has healed much of my fear, brokenness and feelings of inadequacy.

Ministry and Resurrection

Many people can avoid the confrontation with evil if they are not exposed to the suffering, pain and ugliness of the world. However, those who are in the healing professions, the ministering professions, are brought into daily touch with the full gamut of human misery and agony. Doctors, ministers, psychologists, social workers, those working in poverty-stricken countries or the ghettos of our own cities have their faces rubbed in the reality of evil. If these people are not supported by resurrection or hope, we might expect them to suffer burnout and break down—and often they do.

During my years at the University of Notre Dame a group of premedical students came to me and asked me to teach a course on death, dying and suffering. They had looked at the statistics relating to the burnout of doctors and they were alarmed. They discovered that the medical profession had the greatest number of marital failures and divorces of any profession, the greatest number of suicides and psychiatric sicknesses, the greatest use of hard drugs and alcohol. As we wrestled with these facts they came to the conclusion that if they as doctors were to be sensitive to people and not insulate themselves from human need by callous objectivity, they had to find some meaning in the face of all their powerlessness before human sickness, pain and death.

Burnout, with all of its unpleasant symptoms, is also an occupational hazard for psychologists and social workers. Jung used to take one month out of every four to get away to discharge the poisons which he had picked up from his clients. Ministers involved in social action that brings them into touch with human misery often find themselves disillusioned and burned out. In *Ministry Burnout* John Sanford has described well the dangers to those in ministry who do not realize the seriousness of their occupation and do not take time to keep in vital touch with spiritual reality, which alone can sustain us as we deal with the evil in the world. For me it is the resurrected One who gives me strength and enables me to carry on creatively.

Whenever ministers are truly open to human need and are trusted by the community in which they live and work, they will find evil in all its forms. I wish that those who do not realize the reality and power of evil could make the rounds with a conscientious pastor: one night sitting with a family struck by the horror of unexpected death, another day watching beside the bedside of one who has taken an overdose of sleeping pills. Perhaps they might follow her to the county jail where a seemingly respectable man has suddenly gone haywire, leaving him and those related to him facing disaster unless they get the right kind of help or they might listen with him to a family torn by the agony of domestic bitterness. They might hear the despair of someone confessing compulsions that could ruin him or her, or the hopelessness and depression, hate and ugliness which people have longed to share, or the tragedy of fear and guilt.

I thought that it would be different when I went to teach at the university, but I discovered that there also many human beings were suffering far more than most people believe. One college administrator told me that colleges were the loneliest places in the world. My wife and I worked with those priests, nuns and lay people who lived in the dormitories and who were available to students. Until these leaders could talk to one another and share their fears and doubts, the students did not feel comfortable sharing with them. So many of us are afraid of one another and fear that no one can possibly tolerate all of us. I have met very few people who have not had problems with egotism, authority and pride or problems with the passions and sexuality. So few of us are what we desire to be.

And still today I find people at conferences, people who write in agony, friends and people with whom I work in every level of society and every educational background who are struggling through lack of self-worth, guilt, agony, depression and hopelessness. On the collective level, this personal suffering is matched by the specter of world hunger and the threat of nuclear annihilation.

And always there is the darkness and terror within which comes from time to time to me. Conquering evil is not like an algebraic problem which can be solved once and for all. It is a constant battle and I need the continuous presence of the risen One to continue the fight.

I doubt very seriously if I would survive very long without the meaning of the resurrection and the reality of Jesus and his presence. I need this reality so I can have some tangible hope to give to those engulfed in the darkness and agony inflicted by the evil one. If I did not have this I might well be paralyzed in the agony I share with other human beings.

Another Way

There are some people who, while open to the spiritual way, do not seem to be touched with the resurrection message or seem not to need it as much as some of us. They follow a spiritual path of renunciation and denial which is often associated with a view of God or ultimate reality as imageless and beyond our comprehension. It has been called the *via negativa*. It is the spiritual way of denying all passions, love as well as hate. It may involve doubting the reality of this physical world and evil, or seeing evil as simply the absence of good. One of the finest and most human accounts of this way is Gandhi's *An Autobiography: The Story of My Experiments With Truth*. This legitimate and real spiritual way is very much the way of the East, the way of Hinduism and Buddhism. However, some Christian writers also follow this way. Gandhi was certainly a great soul, as the "mahatma" used in his name signifies. His life story is a magnificent example of the spirituality of the *Bhagavad Gita*.

Gandhi and E. Stanley Jones had many discussions of their different religious points of view, and Gandhi himself did not feel a personal need for belief in the resurrection of Jesus. There are some people who have been raised within a culture that is intact and within a family where there is love and concern. Their souls have not been worn thin by evil and pain. It is relatively easy for them to believe in a good and loving God. They pursue the way of perfection and they can attain great spiritual heights.

There are others of us whose personal lives have not been so securely based or who have been robbed of belief and opened to evil by the materialism and disintegration of belief in spiritual reality in Western culture. For these people, as for me, the resurrection is necessary if they are to carry on. I could easily despair if it were *necessary* to have Gandhi's kind of detachment to make progress on the spiritual way. We can work toward perfection with incredible humility like Gandhi or we can accept the saving which has been made possible in the resurrection. When we live truly and deeply in accord with either of these two ways the final results will not be too different, although the paths to that ultimate goal may be very different. What I write in the pages that follow is particularly for those who have found the evil and tragedy of the world more than they can bear; I share with them how the resurrection of Jesus has helped me cope with them. I write also to help those not so troubled by darkness and doubt to understand the need of those it afflicts. This is the *via affirmativa* well described by Charles Williams in *The Figure of Beatrice: A Study in Dante* and in Dante's incomparable *Divine Comedy*. People on each of these ways need to acknowledge the validity of the other and encourage those upon the other way. The important matter is following some religious way, a way which delivers us from evil and helps us toward salvation and eternal life.

Blessed Are the Failures

Few words of Jesus are more difficult to understand and accept than those recorded in Luke in the sermon on the plain, the words following the Beatitudes:

> But alas for you who are rich; you have had your time of
> happiness.

Alas for you who are well fed now; you shall go hungry.
Alas for you who laugh now; you shall mourn and weep.
Alas for you when all speak well of you; just so did their
    fathers treat the false prophets.

What Jesus is telling us in these uncomfortable words is that
very often when people find life going well with them they think
they can manage without God. When we have all we need, when
we are in power and health, when we are admired and happy, we
have a tendency to think we attained that position by our own efforts and that we are not vulnerable to evil. When we have no
God we often believe that we are gods. It is very difficult to be
god and have a saving God at the same time. Jesus is trying to tell
us that to be open to the infinite love and power and mercy of
God, we must realize that we need it; the contented and self-suf-
ficient often forget this.

Dietrich Bonhoeffer was a truly great and courageous man
and a martyr. He was also an author, and in his *Letters From
Prison* he writes that we human beings have come of age and do
not need God to help us along the way. These are strange senti-
ments coming from a prison camp in Nazi Germany. In these
hard words Jesus is telling us just the opposite: we must have
God or our lives shrivel up and blow away. Without God everything eternal in us decays and rots, and we come to death with no
preparation for eternity, even if we have not become soured and
lonely old men and women long before that. Jesus is speaking
spiritual truth. If our medical doctor does not warn us that certain foods do not contain adequate nutrition and that if we live on
them alone we will sicken and die, we would say that this phy-
sician had failed us. The same is true of the soul. A soul nourished only on material things sickens, decays and disintegrates.
This is the basic wisdom of the great religions of humankind. For
me the resurrection is simply the best confirmation of this truth
that history provides and in addition gives us an ever-present
Savior to help us on the way.

Indeed my heart aches for the physically, psychologically
and socially comfortable, for they can lose the pearl of great
price. I fear for the self-satisfied and adequate, the contented
and the complacent, those who think that by their own efforts

they have brought about their condition, those who think they are masters of their fates and captains of their souls, for they can miss the real meaning of life and its eternal significance and joy.

I once had a dream that rain was coming through the roof of a building in which I had a large investment. The beautifully decorated interior was being spoiled. I was distressed by the dream and took it to my friend, James Kirsch, who heaved a sigh of relief and said: "How fortunate you are that your ego is not so thoroughly air-tight that the rain of the spirit cannot get in. The failures of the ego can be the way of access for the spirit." On another occasion he expressed the other side of this same idea, saying that the only type of person he found it difficult to tolerate was the one who didn't even have any neurosis, the one with an iron-clad ego.

What a strange set of Beatitudes Jesus gives us. The blessed are those who are poor (in Luke) or poor in spirit (in Matthew). The fortunate ones are those who go hungry now or who are hungering and thirsting after righteousness and are unsatisfied. The blessed are those who are now weeping and those who are hated, outlawed, insulted and persecuted. Why are they fortunate? Because their inability to handle life by themselves is obvious to them and so they may turn to receive new power through the resurrection and God's grace. Through their very failures they are brought within reach of the new life released through the resurrection.

As I have meditated on these strange Beatitudes and woes I have come to perceive some modern variations:

Blessed are the fearful and the inadequate, for they can be given true confidence.

Blessed are the broken and the confused, for they can be bound up and enlightened.

Blessed are the discouraged and the disillusioned about human things, for the pathway to God can be open to them.

Blessed are the neurotic, for they can find true reality.

Blessed are the depressed, for they can know salvation.

Blessed are the failures in earthly things, because they can be driven to find heavenly things.

These people are the ones who are forced (if they keep up the struggle) to seek and find the redeeming power and love of God which not only sustains, strengthens, and makes whole but also can lift us up out of darkness, defeat evil's attack and give us access to the realms of heaven and eternal victory. The unfortunate men and women of this world are often forced to find what they might have missed had all gone well with them. The resurrection can become the impulse that guides their struggle and the goal toward which they strive.

From a human point of view Jesus was a total failure on Good Friday, but he was resurrected and became the victorious helper of all who turn to him in their inadequacy. Blessed are those who have failed from an earthly point of view and who have turned to the victorious Christ, for they can be transformed in this life and given eternal joy and resurrected life. Knowing that they have been saved not by their own efforts, they usually look with mercy and compassion upon the broken and fragile, the depressed and feeble, the fainthearted and discouraged. How much easier to give unmerited concerned love to others when we have received it in our own defeat.

Easter and Christmas

It is much easier to celebrate Christmas than it is to celebrate Easter, resurrection and atonement. Christmas is a day for the unbroken. It tells of God breaking into this world, to set it aright. Christmas is a family day with a beautiful mother and father, and a child lying in a manger. The coming of God in flesh, the incarnation, speaks of God's incredible love and caring for us bumbling human beings. It speaks of the goodness of human beings. It is the way of those who see the goodness and beauty of the world, those who have not been forced to deal with evil; it hallows our humanity. It reminds us to follow our deepest and best instincts and to love one another as we have been loved.

The resurrection is far different. It touches the divine core within us, gives us the ability to transcend our ordinary humanity at its best, and also transforms our selfishness, our bitterness and evil. The resurrection is like a light too bright to gaze upon.

And as we do look we see that between us and the light there stands a wooden cross bearing all the evil and pain, all the hatred and misery of the world. Sometimes the cross is centered in the very heart of the light so that we cannot look at the light without dealing with the cross; this makes us very uncomfortable.

There are many times in my life when things have been going so well that I can and do forget about the resurrection. When my family is healthy and happy and in harmony, when my friends seek me out, when the world is at peace, when my own anxiety level is low, when there is tranquility and peace in the city streets and country lanes, then I do not linger on Jesus' resurrection. Indeed at these times a large part of me would like to push this event aside until Easter rolls around in the Church year and I have to look at it.

That cross glowing within the light makes me uneasy. It turns life upside down. I don't like to be reminded that the evil one is still lurking in the shadows ready to prey on human evil and turn it to evil's account and so upset the delicate human balance. This part of me does not like to be reminded that most of the important things in my life are not within my power to control, and that I need a power greater than my own to bring me through and give me an eternal foundation. This part of me wants to ignore my need for a divine helper to conquer the darkness that attacks me within and from without, and to deal with death which stands starkly on the horizon waiting to bring dissolution and chaos.

When everything is pleasant on the surface of my life I usually don't want to look below the surface and muddy the water with such thoughts. I would just as soon forget about the resurrection and its bright, searing, transforming light. But it is quite different when life is in tatters and I am faced with outer tragedy or with my own inner ugliness and meanness and pain. Then I cannot do without the resurrection and the rough-hewn cross which it hallows. Then the cross within the creative fire is the greatest comfort I know and I hang onto it with all my might.

When I am sick or bereaved, when my heart is heavy from some outer crisis, or, even worse, when it is in agony and I do not know why, when my friends have deserted or betrayed me, when my enemies appear to have won the day, when nations rise up against nations, when society is breaking down and we are hardly safe in the daytime, let alone at night, then the resurrection is the central reality which keeps me going.

Some subjects can be treated analytically, unemotionally, but some subjects need to be treated with passion. When my life has been saved again and again, a polite thank you is not enough. When I see a ship going down against the rocks and there is a way to rescue it, and people will not listen, sometimes I must cry out with passion. One poem that I learned as a child always seemed wrong—these words from Henley's "Invictus":

> It matters not how strait the gate,
>   How charged with punishments the scroll,
> I am the master of my fate,
>   I am the captain of my soul.

I do not have an unconquerable soul. In the storms of life I will go under and disintegrate without the one who has conquered evil and death. If I am the only master of my fate and captain of my soul I am lost and a failure, but there is one who will captain my soul and bring me to a fate better than I had dreamed possible, if I will allow it. I truly feel sorry for those who think they are equal to life through their own secular power. They are denied the ultimate confidence.

My relationship with the resurrection and the resurrected One is not a matter of piety and religious good works. Meditation on the meaning of Jesus' rising from the dead and fellowship with the victorious Christ are not a matter of adding a religious savor to my life, but rather a matter of survival. Keeping in touch with this reality is the only way I know of dealing with the evil which attacks people from within their souls and also in the outer world. It is the only way I know to move toward the growth and transformation that are God's destiny for us all.

It is not enough to express this experience with passion. I must now look at why this reality transforms us. What happened on the first Easter? Who was this person who died and rose again? Why does it make such a difference to so many?

2.

Who Was This Man?

Hundreds of thousands of men and women have been tortured and died in the sad chronicles of human history. Many died with nobility and courage. It would be difficult even to estimate how many thousands Rome nailed to crosses to be examples for its subject people. And yet few of them are remembered and none of them has attracted even a fraction of the interest or attention that Jesus of Nazareth has attracted. The courageous way Jesus endured is an important part of that total picture, but it does not explain why men and women for twenty centuries have turned to the crucified Christ and been transformed.

And there are also many stories of resurrection. People supposedly genuinely dead have returned to life and yet we hear little or nothing of them later. The New Testament records the raising of Lazarus and yet I know of no Lazarians, followers of this raised one. Peter on his journeys to visit the Christian brothers and sisters came to Lydia and found that one of their most beloved members, Tabitha, had died; he raised her from the dead and yet there is no sect of Tabithians. There were no followers of the son of the widow of Nain or of Jairus' daughter, who were also raised.

There were gods who died and rose again in Asia Minor and Egypt and India. Few people believe that Ganesha, the son of Parvati and Shiva, was an historical person, but he is the one most worshiped in much popular Hinduism. His father cut off his head in anger and brought him back to life with an elephant's head. Throughout the Roman Empire there were great festivals celebrating the rising of Adonis and Attis and Osiris and many

people were deeply touched by them, but they were not historical figures. It was almost as if the religious dreams and hopes for
resurrecting power were finally realized in the historical person
of the risen Jesus. What happened in the life and resurrection of
Jesus which makes so much difference? Why was it so significant?

There are many different kinds of people in our world.
There are some who do not need to understand; all they need to
do is to experience being pulled up out of the pit and that is
enough. But there are others who truly need to understand what
happened at the resurrection of Jesus—why it happened, how it
happened, and why it makes so much difference. If we are to
share the incredible transforming and redeeming power of this
risen One with all kinds of people, we need to be able to explain
why it is important and what it says about the nature of the universe. Then we can bring the depth of our lives into harmony
with the love that made the resurrection possible. But first of all,
what actually happened?

The Resurrection

Nearly two thousand years ago some very strange things
took place in one of the far-off provinces of the Empire of Rome.
A man of magnetic personal appeal began to proclaim that the
long awaited Kingdom of heaven, the Kingdom of God, was at
hand. The King and the Kingdom were characterized by over-
flowing, unbounded self-giving love and mercy. This Kingdom
was penetrating our world and was available to humans now.
This man, Jesus of Nazareth, brought people to an experience of
that Kingdom right here on earth. He believed that ordinary
mortals could converse with this Father-like God and King. Jesus
also taught great crowds that they needed to treat other women
and men now as they would if they found themselves in that
heavenly Kingdom; only thus could they experience that Kingdom now. However, the full and total experience of this Kingdom only took place after death, in eternity.

Jesus had no credentials except the authority with which he
spoke and taught and healed. He was not a part of the religious

hierarchy of his people. He came from an impoverished peasant background in a subject country. He was the son of a carpenter and was a skilled carpenter himself. His mother was a young village maiden. To help him spread his message he gathered together a motley group of disciples, fishermen, tax collectors, and peasants. They lived together and tried to experience the Kingdom of God here on earth. After he had trained them, he sent them out to spread the good news that a new era had dawned. These disciples discovered that they could preach and teach and heal in much the same way the master did. Jesus also taught that there were forces in the universe which were trying to resist the coming of the Kingdom. Evil was a reality in God's world and it wished to scatter misery and hatred, divisiveness and death, sin and corruption among us human beings. Even more radical was Jesus' treatment of women and children; he viewed them as having the same value and religious capacities as men, and invited them into his fellowship. Jesus was the only major religious leader in history to value them in this way.

Jesus' actions reveal a person who practiced what he preached. His medium and his message were the same. He spoke out against anything which broke or marred the human spirit. He stood up for and championed the poor, the rejected, tax collectors, prostitutes, the sick and all outcasts. He challenged the religious leaders of his country because they did not minister to these people who needed religious help the most. The Nazarene lived the message of love that he proclaimed. He was all of one piece. In addition to all this, an uncanny power appeared to flow from him and reinforced the power of his words. In this power he reached out to the physically and mentally ill and healed them. It was reported that he even raised the dead.

Jesus lived in a politically sensitive area. The Jewish people were resistive under the power of Rome. Many times the people rose in armed rebellion, and each time Rome clamped down more severely on this conquered nation. Jesus' popularity and his disregard for some of the religious traditions of his people threatened the temple authorities. On one of the great festival days he descended upon the very temple precincts and threw out the money changers and those who were buying and selling animals for sacrifices. He called the place a den of thieves. The religious leaders of his people were frightened that he might instigate another revolt and cause them to lose what little independence they had. They seized him, then met and accused him of blasphemy and political subversion. They turned him over to the Roman governor, Pontius Pilate. Jesus of Nazareth was condemned to die. After torture they nailed him to a cross where he hung in agony until he died. Above his head was a placard telling the crime for which he was executed: Jesus of Nazareth, King of the Jews.

That good men and women have been liquidated by arbitrary civil authority is not new or surprising. Some of the finest and most deeply religious people have been destroyed because they were a nuisance to the military or to political power. From the dawn of history up to the present, evil forces have often destroyed the good. But Jesus the Nazarene did not stay dead. First a few and then an increasing number claimed that he had risen from the dead and had come to meet with them. He had conquered death and come to give his disciples and friends a new vision of life and a new power with which to cope with it. Even after he no longer appeared in bodily form, his disciples maintained that he was still present to them and shared with them a portion of his life and spirit. His rabbit-hearted followers had fled from him on the night he was betrayed and captured. Some of them had denied that they knew him. These people were transformed by their encounter with the resurrected Jesus. These weak-kneed and cowardly followers became a band of fearless men and women who brought a new religious faith to birth against the greatest odds. In the power of their transformation, their conviction and their love these men and women conquered the Roman Empire which had tried to snuff out the faith they proclaimed. Most of the original band of disciples died witnessing to their faith. Those who had met and known the risen Jesus were no longer afraid, even in death. They believed that death and evil had been defeated and were no longer of ultimate significance. They maintained that the resurrection of Jesus was the basis and foundation for their transformation, their lack of fear, their freedom, their love and their victorious and contagious joy. They abandoned the Jewish sabbath as their weekly holy day and began to celebrate Sunday, the first day of the week, the day of the resurrection. This was not so much a day of total rest as a celebration in gratitude for Jesus' rising from the dead.

Their conviction that the risen Jesus was among them constitutes one of the basic problems of New Testament biblical criticism. For the Gospel authors the risen Jesus was so real and present that they did not distinguish clearly between the actual historical record and their post-resurrection encounters with Jesus. They also believed that Jesus had sent the Holy Spirit among them and within them, and this empowered them to carry on the ministry of good news, power and transformation their master had begun.

This kind of experience did not cease with the death of the original followers of Jesus. Starting with Saul men and women continued to experience the risen Jesus and were transformed by that encounter. The list of those transformed by the risen Christ is nearly endless: Gregory of Nazianzen, Basil the Great, Ambrose, Augustine, Martin of Tours, Francis of Assisi, Dante, Catherine of Genoa, Ignatius of Loyola, John Bunyan, John Wesley, Martin Luther King, and the multitude described by William James in *The Varieties of Religious Experience*. These people have told much the same story of being lost and in agony, of being rescued by the risen Christ from bondage to themselves and to evil, and of being brought to God's love, a love that they in no way deserved.

A few days ago I received the following letter from someone I had helped to find this reality: "I remember my first meeting with you—on your way out the door of the library into the bitter February cold you turned to me and said: 'The Christ is real.' It startled me, because I didn't feel you were speaking out of the usual 'religious' attitude. I sensed that you *knew* what you were talking about. And that hope connected with something deep in me. Our mutual friend had a similar reaction when he first met you. You were able to connect both of us to that reality because you had known it through your own struggle." The Christ, the risen One, is real, and he can touch our lives and help us through our inner and outer lostness as much today as in the time of the apostles and New Testament authors. But why is the resurrection so important?

A Drama and an Arch

I have come to see the resurrection as the central act of the great cosmic drama, the drama of God creating and redeeming the world. The drama has seven acts, and each of them is essential to an appreciation of the full magnitude of God's loving action. Let me sketch out the seven acts.

Act I—An incomplete creation, magnificent but incomplete. God creates heaven and earth (the spiritual world and the physical world) and it is good. God creates because he loves, but some of the heavenly host feel that they are as good as God. They go their own way and so evil breaks forth into our universe.

Act II—Creation continues in incarnation. God comes into this world to complete creation and to provide a way in which creation might always continue. God becomes a human being and dwells among us to deliver our world from evil.

Act III—Manifestation. God reveals his nature to the world *in the world* by living as an ordinary baby, child and adolescent. As an adult he begins to preach, teach and heal, to reveal the self-giving, unbounded love which is the essence of God and the heart of all reality. God in Jesus meets evil on the cross and submits to it.

Act IV—Resurrection. The way of love and non-violence is victoriously affirmed. Jesus rises from the dead and comes to his defeated and despairing followers. They are transformed and become victorious too.

Act V—Ascension. Jesus as a human being resumes his eternal cosmic status and is now available in all time and space.

Act VI—Pentecost. The risen and cosmic Christ sends the Spirit in a new way upon those who will receive it. A new era opens for human beings.

Act VII—Response. Our part in this drama is responding to the limitless divine love, mercy and healing power. The drama is not truly complete until we humans respond and allow the cosmic victory to be an earthly and human one.

Many Christians are concerned only with one act of the play and not with all seven. Some write of creation theology and do not see that creation is only completed in the death and resurrection of Jesus, in salvation. Some find only the incarnation necessary. Other people suffer needlessly by concentrating only on the suffering and crucifixion of Jesus. They fail to move on to resurrection. They get caught in the tragedy and pain of Golgotha. Some of them try to imitate his suffering and don't know how to move on to the joy and peace and gratitude of resurrection. Still others emphasize Pentecost and fail to realize that Pentecost only makes sense in terms of the previous five acts of the drama. Still others know well the first six acts and fail to make them a part of their lives.

A play is a unitary whole and we do violence to it if we deal with only one act or with several. The resurrection is indeed the central act of the drama, but it manifests its full meaning only when we look at creation and evil in the created world, as we pause in adoration at God's self-emptying in the birth in Bethlehem. Resurrection only achieves its true significance when we see it as the resurrection of a human being (yes, and more than a human being) who lived, taught, healed and died as he did. The resurrection only makes sense as the central act and action of the divine drama with six other acts. No one of these six acts reaches its full and total meaning except in terms of the resurrection and the other five acts as well.

For some people the image of an arch may make more sense. The Christian story can be seen as a monumental arch of seven great stones. The two bottom stones rest upon the earth. There is the stone of incomplete creation and corresponding to it on the other side is our response. The arch falls without creation and response. And then there is the stone of incarnation, of God breaking into the world to finish creation. Opposite to that stone is Pentecost in which there is still another pouring out of God into the world in the gift to human beings of new dimensions of the divine love and power. And then there are two curved stones, one curving into full participation in the earth and its evil and ending in crucifixion. The other stone is curved and leads this one who has been victorious back into the reality of cosmic glory, the ascension, a parting at which there was no grief. The keystone holds any arch together, and the resurrection as the keystone does exactly this. Without the raising of Jesus the whole arch ends as a jumble of broken stones upon the ground. Yet looking at the keystone alone, it seems a strange stone and we wonder what value or meaning it can have. The resurrection without the rest of the stones of the arch has little significance. The arch is an integral whole just like the drama.

Let us look together at these seven different elements in the cosmic Christian drama, the seven stones in the arch of Christian faith. I shall deal with six of these actions rather briefly, just enough to establish their essential importance. I shall treat the resurrection more fully, but this fuller treatment only makes sense within the setting God has provided for it.

3.

Incomplete Creation

The subject of evil could fill many books. This is not the place to examine all the ramifications of this difficult problem. However, if we are to understand the significance of the resurrection of Jesus we need to see that it took place in a world in which evil sometimes prospers and the good are often destroyed. In the Old Testament we hear this anguished cry from the Psalms to Jeremiah, from Job to Ezekiel.[1]

One of the most basic ideas of Judaism, Christianity and Islam is that God created the world out of nothing and what he created was good. In Genesis after God finished his creating activity and before he rested on the seventh day we find these words: "So it was; and God saw all that he had made, and it was very good. Evening came, and morning came, a sixth day." The world springs out of the mind and action of God. But that leaves us with a big problem: if this is so, why all the agony and suffering, the tragedy and hatred, the ugliness and selfishness in the world?

First we should realize that this biblical point of view is quite different from other ways of looking at the world. Most of the religions that arose in India tell us that this physical world and the evil and misery, poverty and warfare in it are not ultimately real. They are *maya* or illusion. When we become enlightened, we are no longer deceived by illusion and then evil no longer afflicts us. Some years ago I drove from New Delhi to Agra one unbearable summer day. The road was crowded with millions of people, cows, elephants, camels, and bullocks. Poverty and filth were everywhere. The problems seemed unsolvable, and I could cer-

37

tainly see why Buddha accepted the Hindu solution, declaring
this monstrosity an illusion.

At the opposite pole we find the solution of atheistic or agnostic materialism. The problem of evil is solved by stating that
there is no problem. The whole mess is the natural result of pure
chance, bubbling mud pots and blind genes creating human
beings to perpetuate themselves. There is no more reason to be
surprised by evil than by good; both are just chance happenings
in a meaningless whole. From this point of view the very words
good and evil have little meaning.

Another view of the universe was very common when Jesus
and Christianity were born into the world—the gnostic understanding of evil. In this view of the universe there were two gods.
One created the spiritual world, known as the pleroma, the
blessedness of pure ecstatic spirituality; then there was an evil
god, a demiurge, who created the physical world, and this world
was irredeemably evil. In a cosmic catastrophe the spiritual
world blew up and fragments of spirit became imbedded in the
ugly nastiness of matter, and from this union human beings resulted. The only way of salvation was asceticism, which denied
physical desire and so separated us out of our connection with
matter. The worst sin was sexuality, which resulted in concep-
tion and thus brought more spirit into union with matter.
Against this point of view the early Church Fathers continuously
warred because it devalued the physical world, separated the
New Testament from the Old Testament and made the incarnation only apparent. This was the *dualism* of Mani and his followers. Many thinkers wanted to base Christian theology on this
point of view. It has, unfortunately, come down into Christianity
through many sources, and particularly through Augustine, who
for years was a peripheral member of the Manicheans.

The dualism of the ancient Persians, associated with the
name of Zoroaster, was quite different from gnosticism, but still
worlds away from Judaism and Christianity. In that point of
view there were two gods, one evil and one good, who were powerful in both the spiritual domain and the physical one. Indeed
human beings helped secure the final victory of the god of light as
they followed the way of kindness, goodness, justice and truth.
They gave power to the forces of evil as they participated in mur-

der, lying, cruelty and other evils. Christianity and Christians could not accept this solution either because human beings were saving themselves rather than being saved by the victory of Jesus.

If, however, God made the world and it was good, where did evil come from? Many different answers have been offered. Some Christian thinkers, following Aristotle, suggest that the evil in the world is merely the accidental lack of perfection in the universe, the inevitable result of the creative process. Most Scholastic thinkers adopted this point of view. And then there is the doctrine of the fall where humans beguiled by the serpent decided to make themselves equal with God and were banished from the garden. But this leaves us with the question: Where did the serpent come from? What is the origin of that deceiving and corrupting reality which drags us into rebellion and banishment from God's presence?

There is yet another way of looking at the persistent problem of evil, one which is found in the New Testament, in the vital early Church, in Dante, and which has emerged in recent years in the thinking of many popular modern Christian writers. According to this point of view ultimate reality cannot be described in a purely analytical way. Spiritual reality does not dissolve into intellectual formulae any more than material reality does. In order to describe the ultimate nature of reality we must use symbols, images, pictures and poetry. Charles Williams, C.S. Lewis and other writers, influenced by Owen Barfield, came to see that symbolism, poetry, myth and story are not an inferior form of language, but actually reveal the nature of reality better than anything else. A myth is not, as Bultmann described it, a story we make up to fill in the gaps of our knowledge, but rather a story which reveals the nature and structure of spiritual reality.[2] The basic idea of creation in this viewpoint is that God created the world and it was good, but something went astray. I am quite sure that God was well aware that something might go astray when spiritual beings were created with freedom, but Love desires real love in return and this can only come from free individuals. God risked evil that love might be born. God undoubtedly realized that another stage of creation would probably be necessary in which evil would be defeated in an ultimate sense. Creation required the development of human beings who would be able to respond to God when this later phase of creation took place.

A cosmic drama is revealed in both John's Book of Revelation and in Dante's expansion of the story. In the former we find this passage: "Then war broke out in heaven. Michael and his angels waged war upon the dragon. The dragon and his angels fought, but they had not the strength to win, and no foothold was left them in heaven. So the great dragon was thrown down, that serpent of old that led the whole world astray, whose name is Satan, or the devil—thrown down to the earth, and his angels with him" (Rev 12:7ff). This was the beginning of the trouble in heaven and on earth.

The basic problem was that Lucifer, Satan, the dragon, was created free. He was free to follow God's way or another. (It should be noted that the evil one no more than God can be seen as purely masculine.) What a wonderful and terrible thing freedom is. Once we are truly free we can choose God's way of patient self-giving love or something else. When we are free we are totally responsible. Lucifer (light-bringer) was one of the brightest and best of the children of the morning, one of the greatest and most capable of the created angels. He surveyed all of creation and came to the conclusion that God's way of love was unrealistic. God's was no way to run a universe. Satan was an efficiency expert, cold and calculating, and decided for the way of power. Like many adolescents Lucifer didn't know how to use his freedom. Along with a batch of "advanced, realistic" angels he rebelled against God and tried to take over heaven. Whenever we consciously or unconsciously decide that our way is better than God's way we join the Satanic fellowship. We don't have to attend a black mass to join up.

God and good, however, were not that easily defeated. St. Michael and his angels threw Satan out of heaven. In a universe where the earth is the center of all things, there was only one place to go when thrown out of heaven—down to earth. This was the beginning of our trouble. This also explains the serpent in the garden and the reason for the feasts of St. Michael and All Angels. The same story is told in another way by Charles Williams in his novel *War in Heaven*.

Dante develops the story further as is shown in the following diagrams. Dante, and the educated people of his time, believed that the cosmos was quite understandable. There were ten heavens surrounding the earth; thus Satan fell a long distance and hit the earth with such an impact that he created a great concavity in the earth known as hell. Satan penetrated to the very center of the earth where he is frozen in a cake of ice, the perfect symbol of the perfect isolation of those who think that their way of doing things is superior to that of God. Buzzing around in the concavity are the fallen angel-demons of heaven thrown out with Satan. They also flit around the earth trying to draw human beings into their following.

The first diagram shows the ten levels of heaven, the second one the state of the earth after this heavenly and earthly tragedy.[3] Dante realized that the picture he painted in incomparable Italian poetry was symbolic and not astronomically accurate. The picture presented an account of how evil came to be. However, less sophisticated men and women did take the diagrams literally, and when it was shown that the earth was not the physical center of the universe and that hell was not "down there," their whole religious meaning collapsed and human beings were left without an understanding of evil and how it came into God's world. Then they either rejected the idea of evil entirely if they were of a scientific mind, or they became overwhelmed by it and went out on witch hunts, an unfortunate pastime of the late Christian Middle Ages.

But we can offer a further development of the story in which the heavenly and earthly aspects of creation meet and mingle. Both are real. In the tragic fall of the brightest and best of the children of the morning, Satan lost his real power in the heavenly sphere and entered the physical terrain and has been bedeviling human beings ever since. Something had to be done without violating the freedom of those involved. The Book of Revelation goes on and anticipates several more acts of the divine drama we are describing. "Then I heard a voice in heaven proclaiming aloud: 'This is the hour of victory for our God, the hour of his sovereignty and power, when his Christ comes to his rightful rule! For the accuser of our brothers is overthrown, who day and

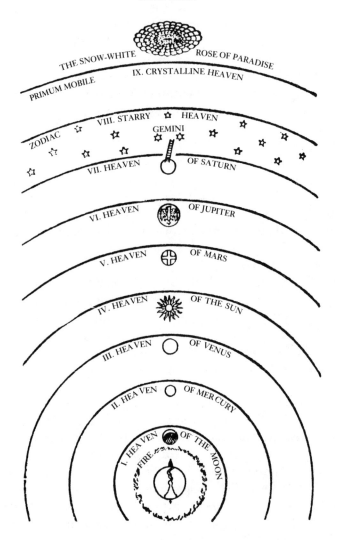

X. EMPYREAN

THE SNOW-WHITE ROSE OF PARADISE

PRIMUM MOBILE IX. CRYSTALLINE HEAVEN

ZODIAC VIII. STARRY ☆ HEAVEN
GEMINI
VII. HEAVEN OF SATURN

VI. HEAVEN OF JUPITER

V. HEAVEN OF MARS

IV. HEAVEN OF THE SUN

III. HEAVEN OF VENUS

II. HEAVEN OF MERCURY

I. HEAVEN OF THE MOON
FIRE

GENERAL VIEW OF PARADISE

42

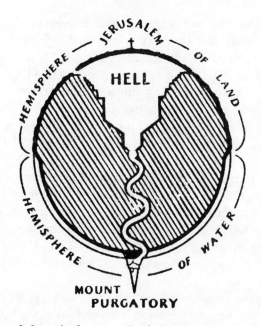

night accused them before our God. By the sacrifice of the Lamb they have conquered him and by the testimony which they uttered, for they did not hold their lives too dear to lay them down' " (Rev 12:10ff).

The basic idea of this author and many other apostolic writers was that human beings had fallen into bondage to the evil one and his minions and that somehow in Christ's birth, living, preaching, dying, resurrection, ascension and the coming of the Holy Spirit we human beings were freed from this bondage. This belief was known as the ransom theory of atonement. Gustav Aulén demonstrates clearly in *Christus Victor* that this was the most common early Christian belief about how evil had gained its place in the world and how it was defeated so that it no longer had ultimate power. People *experienced* freedom from bondage in their encounter with the loving power of the risen Christ. The victorious confidence that evil was defeated is found in the New Testament and in all the major orthodox Christian writers for the next eight or nine hundred years.

Paul writes to the Galatians: "Formerly, when you did not acknowledge God, you were slaves of beings which in their nature are no gods. But now that you do acknowledge God—or

rather, now that he has acknowledged you—how can you turn
back to the mean and beggarly spirits of the elements? Do you
propose to enter their service all over again? (Gal 4:8–9). The
First Epistle of Peter brings the same message: "Baptism is not
the washing away of bodily pollution, but the appeal made to
God by a good conscience; and it brings salvation through the
resurrection of Jesus Christ, who entered heaven after receiving
the submission of angelic authorities and powers, and is now at
the right hand of God (1 Pet 3:21–22). Again in Romans, Paul
writes the passage which had been helpful to so many and is often
read at funerals: "For I am convinced that there is nothing in
death or life, in the realm of spirits or superhuman powers, in the
forces of the universe, in heights or depths—nothing in all creation that can separate us from the love of God in Christ Jesus our
Lord" (Rom 8:38–39). This is not just nice poetry; it is spiritual
realism.

But, many people will ask, isn't this all very pre-modern? I
don't think so. The very modern psychiatrist C.G. Jung and his
followers opened my eyes and heart to the fact that evil is real,
must be faced and can be overcome. Jung and Fr. Victor White
had many discussions on the problem of evil, and Fr. White expresses much of Jung's view of the subject in his book, *God and the
Unconscious*. He remarks that the theologian and the psychologist,
in talking about these experiences, "each describes an observed
occurrence from a different view-point," and that each is refer-
ring to the same phenomenon. He goes on with these reflections:

> In the pages of the New Testament, Satan and the devils may
> be said to be fairly ubiquitous from the beginning to the end.
> The polite efforts of nineteenth-century Liberal criticism to
> exorcise the demons from the New Testament, to explain
> away its more "devilish" passages as a later and superstitious
> adulteration of the pure ethical milk of the Gospel, or at least
> to apologize for them as an unimportant concession to con-
> temporary illusions, have proved a dismal failure. Even the
> most radical criticism of *Formgeschichte* holds that these pas-
> sages belong to the most primitive strata, the essential core,
> of the evangelical tradition. Especially since Schweitzer and
> Otto, it has become difficult to read the Gospels at all other-
> wise than as an account of the struggle between the *de jure*

Reign of God and the *de facto* Reign of Satan—the actual "prince" or "god" of this world over human hearts, minds and affairs. "The devil," Tertullian will say, with customary exaggeration and insight, "is fully known only to Christians." The coming of Christ itself evokes the spirit of anti-Christ; only when the full light shines in the darkness is the intensity of the darkness made manifest. Not only the words and actions of Christ as related in the Gospels, but also the Epistles, and still more obviously the Apocalypse, are largely unintelligible except on the supposition of the reality and activity of Satan and other malevolent spirits.[4]

Through friendship and work with some of Jung's followers I discovered the reality of evil within me and around me. About then I was also introduced to the seven novels of Charles Williams and evil became even more real. I realized that because something was spiritual did not mean it was good; indeed in order to be truly evil, destructiveness had to have its source in spiritual evil. I also read the children's stories of C.S. Lewis and Tolkien's trilogy. Evil began to have a face for me. When I read the Dorothy Sayers translation of Dante's *Divine Comedy* I understood how deeply these modern Christian writers had drunk of the depth of the Christian message. As I studied the Lord's Prayer in Greek I realized that in this version (and we have none earlier in Aramaic) we are told to ask that we be delivered not from evil, but from "the evil one." When I asked a member of the joint liturgical commission why this translation was not used in our common liturgies, he acknowledged that "the evil one" correctly translated the Greek word and suggested that the commission was afraid that the people did not believe in such a reality.

Only those who do not understand the essential message of Christianity and the resurrection need to fear evil or the demonic. We don't have to look for demons behind every garage or under every bed, because these forces have been defeated. In the power and love of Christ we have the support of the one who vanquished them and so have no reason to be afraid of them. Because these destructive realities are real does not mean they are concrete little red creatures with pitchforks and barbed tails.

Sometimes when I turn inward to deal with the tension and conflict within me I see a vista with my inner eye. Before me is a

deep valley with great mountain ranges on either side. One of
them, higher than the high Sierras, glistens with light. Near the
top is a jewel-like castle wherein the risen Christ and the heavenly host dwell, awaiting the call of those in need. On the other
side of the valley is a dark range, shrouded in black and threat-
ening thunderheads. Here thunder echoes, while lightning
flashes reveal the battlements of a grim black stronghold.

On the floor of the valley are many peasant huts where people dwell. One of them is mine, and I often watch and wait, fearful that the forces of evil will swoop down from the dark towers.
And sometimes they come so stealthily that they capture me before I know what is happening. I am powerless to stand against
them. When they attack, if I do not call for help greater than my
own, I am either laid low or dragged away into the dungeons in
the caverns beneath the dismal fortresses. I am saved from these
demonic, destructive powers only when I turn toward the bright
castle, remember that the Christ has defeated the forces of evil,
and call out for help. I wish it were not so, but I have discovered
that the powers of light and peace and strength seldom offer their
help to us human beings unless we cry out and ask for it directly.

The forces of evil keep trying to trick me and drag me into
their places of dark power. When I am a captive I realize that I
cannot defeat evil by myself. I am lost until I turn to the risen Jesus and his angel hosts for help. Very few of us seek God simply
because we are so pure and holy and religious. Generally we seek
the resurrected One because we are forced to, because we realize
that we can't stand against the might of evil unless we do. We will
be destroyed without this help. How often this is the message of
the Psalms.

Many modern men and women suddenly awaken (often in
middle life) to realize that they are lost and need help. Their place
is in the great gulf between these powers. The risen One is there
to help us the moment we realize that we cannot help ourselves.

Before the divine drama of resurrection was enacted human
beings had little sure evidence that we who were so stained with
darkness could reach out to the light and be delivered from evil.
Evil was in the world and had brought the great majority of humankind into its bondage. Human beings were helpless, and
then in the fullness of time God took pity upon us and came

among us to deliver us from evil. The very being of God, the Logos, the Word, became a human being and was born as a baby in Bethlehem. Creation was completed. This brings us to the second act of God's drama. The tragedy was to be redeemed and so became the great drama of salvation. Dante called his play in Italian *The Comedy*. A real comedy is a tragedy redeemed.

4.

Creation Continued

If we were to follow the order of the development of Christian tradition in the early Church, we would treat the incarnation, the coming of God in the flesh, *after* our discussion of the historical life and teaching of Jesus and his rising from the dead. For, although there were clues in the truly marvelous and unfathomable life and teachings of Jesus that suggested he was no ordinary human being, it was the rising of this God-like figure from a noble death on a cross that brought home to his disciples and other followers that they had been in fellowship with God incarnate.

The victorious presence of the death-conquering Jesus sustained the members of the early Church through incredibly difficult trials. The only way they could make sense of what they had *experienced* was to believe that God had appeared among them as one of them. They began to think about how this had occurred. If, indeed, God had broken into the world in this amazing person, when and how did it happen? How was such a thing possible? Pagan religions gave many examples of gods becoming men or women or even appearing to mortals disguised as animals. However, the coming of Jesus into the world was a new twist on these old stories. Three of the Gospels begin with an account of the birth of God into the world that God had created. In the pages to come I will be following the tradition while at the same time calling attention to the fact that the importance of the incarnation only became apparent after the crucifixion and resurrection took place.

How can a mere mortal speak adequately of God breaking into history and time and space as a human being? God's entering

48

into the divine creation staggers the mind and the imagination. Yet this is the central statement of Act II of the cosmic drama. When I really engage this idea it is so overwhelming that it seems to be the whole drama in itself and I need to remind myself that there are five more acts.

And then I think of trying to present this incredible idea to a world which, on the whole, lives as though the material world of meaningless particles and forces was the only important and significant reality. From this point of view there is no realm of meaning from which anything can break in, let alone a divine love which created us and yearns to receive our love. How can one speak with any power of conviction to this world?

Sometimes a story can help when rational and logical statements appear to say so little. Kierkegaard tried to describe incarnation by telling the story of a powerful ruler who wanted to be honestly related to and loved by his subjects. Let us take his idea and imagine such a ruler of great power living in a vast, magnificent, cultured, rich and powerful country near a tiny country which had long before declared its independence from the empire. A number of powerful nobles in the empire had revolted. They were subdued and banished, and they fled to the little principality and took over its entire life. These nobles even convinced the populace that the great empire did not exist. The sovereign, however, did not abandon the citizens of the rebellious nation and still sent disguised agents of mercy and caring into the country. Sometimes they operated successfully without being known because they were hidden, simple people. But sometimes they were discovered and then they were usually mocked, belittled and destroyed. Some of them were called prophets and teachers.

At the appropriate time the ruler thought of a plan: "These people may have grown enough through their misery and the teaching of my agents to be able now to receive me. Perhaps they can know how much I love them and how much I desire their love and wholeness. I could invade the country and take charge, but the human heart is a fortress of freedom and this would not bring them freely to me. No, instead I will go among them as one of them. I will empty myself of my power, my might, my majesty and become as the least of them. Maybe then they will realize how my heart burns for them, how deeply I am touched by their disease and suffering, by their wars and pettiness."

The sovereign was incredibly wise, and, further, possessed perfectly all the qualities which had been separately given to men and women in that country. Because of his absolute fullness of being, he knew that it was impossible to appear among the citizens of the rebellious nation as he truly was because then they would be overawed by his power and glory, and would likely turn to this majesty for reasons other than love. The people of that nation would be so impressed by his androgynous perfection and personal magnificence that these qualities would have to be left behind. The ruler decided to enter the country in total disguise. He was convinced that by living a simple life among those people they would eventually be attracted by his love and that love would effectively turn their minds and their hearts away from the evil nobles. But the great one also knew that such an enormous act of love would not at first win an overwhelmingly positive response. He knew clearly and in detail what it would cost to reach out and touch the hearts of those rebellious citizens. And with great wisdom the ruler also knew that in order to defeat the evil nobles, the *de facto* rulers of that rebellious land, he would eventually have to fight a mighty battle, because the evil nobles would come to suspect and then to know definitely that their enemy had entered their country in disguise. Once they came to know his presence in their land they would fight to their dying breaths. Should they hear of the plans before he entered the country they would do everything they could to prevent the entrance. For this reason he knew that a triumphal procession or an invasion would not work. He decided to enter the country in disguise, as an ordinary man among men, because coming as a woman would have been futile in that world. The battle against the evil nobles would be fought, insofar as was possible, on the ruler's own terms and in a loving, self-sacrificing way. The sovereign prepared to enter the rebellious kingdom with full knowledge that such evil powers would make every attempt to prevent any change in their control of the situation.

C.S. Lewis writes wisely on the subject of evil in the world invaded by the powerful loving one, the same evil which is encountered in our own world. "To be sure, the morbid inquisitiveness about such being [the powers of evil], which led our ancestors to a pseudo-science of Demonology, is to be sternly discouraged; our attitude should be that of the sensible citizen in wartime who believes that there are enemy spies in our midst but disbelieves nearly every particular spy story. We must limit ourselves to the general statement that beings in a different, and higher, 'Nature' which is *partially* interlocked with ours have, like men, fallen and have tampered with things inside our frontiers. The doctrine, besides proving itself fruitful of good in each man's spiritual life, helps to protect us from shallowly optimistic or pessimistic views of Nature."[1]

The story of the emperor is not unlike another story set down in the pages of the New Testament. There was a young Jewish girl by the name of Mary living in the unimportant village of Nazareth in the minor province of Palestine during the reign of Caesar Augustus when Quirinius was governor of Syria and Herod was ruler in Jerusalem. A divine messenger appeared to this young woman while she was at prayer and announced to her that she would conceive and bear a son, a child, whom she should name Jesus. This son would be great and would be called "Son of the Most High." He would establish a new Kingdom which would last forever. Mary was startled and fearful. She was engaged to be married to Joseph who lived in the same village, and she wondered how such a thing could happen. The messenger told her that the Holy Spirit would come upon her and the power of the Most High would overshadow her. Mary was truly devout and replied: "Here am I. I am the Lord's servant; as you have spoken, so be it." Mary came from a people and a family who still believed that there was another, a heavenly Kingdom and that the only true allegiance belonged to God, the infinite and loving monarch of that land.

The powers of evil were excellent discerners of spirits and realized that a very dangerous invasion had taken place. They immediately went into action. First of all they attacked Joseph. He was a fine, upright and very human man. When Mary told him her story he was at first incredulous, but when it became evident that she was indeed pregnant, he was quite upset. We must not be too harsh in our judgment of Joseph. What would most of us men do, even the best, if our fiancées came to us and informed us that they were indeed pregnant by the Holy Spirit? W. H. Auden has portrayed the poignant quality of these struggles in his Christmas play *For the Time Being*. It took the invasion of another divine messenger to bring Joseph around. An angelic being appeared to him in a dream and confirmed everything that Mary had said. They lived on in Nazareth amid the gossip of the villagers until they were forced to go to Bethlehem for the census which the Roman authorities had decreed. What a magnificent man and human being Joseph became as he supported Mary during the long months that dragged on.

To many of us the idea of bearing such a divine child appears quite a romantic notion, but the reality was far from easy. The powers of evil did everything they could to abort the divine plan. First came the long journey of the pregnant woman and her husband from Nazareth to Bethlehem in the dead of winter. Joseph and Mary were poor and without connections. It was difficult to find places to stay along the way, and when they came to their destination there was no room in the Bethlehem inn. And so the holy child was not born in a palace with servants and comforts and received on a silken pillow. He was not born in a well-swept room in the inn with an attendant to help. The divine child was not even born in the cozy home of some kindly villager with a motherly peasant bustling about. The child who ushered in a new age and completed creation was born in a stable—a rough, crude, dirty, foul-smelling Oriental stable.

It is best not to think too imaginatively about that stable. It was built for the ox and the ass, and it housed them none too comfortably. It was about as humble a place as we can imagine. This was all that these strangers, vagabonds from the world's point of view, could find. There is a legend that many strangers came out of the cold, dark night into the stable's dismal shelter to rest and then go their way. A runaway shepherd stopped there one night. He had killed and robbed his cruel master. He hid in the stable and the stable did not turn him out. Another night a prostitute came, weary of the manifold perversions that she endured, and rested quietly upon the straw. A drunken soldier slipped into the stable on still another night and slept off his drunk.

The very Creator of heaven and earth was born in this stable. The most lowly place was selected so that the union with humanity would be total and the disguise would be complete. No human being could claim a humbler birth, and so no derelict, no starving peasant, no broken soul could be excluded from the emptying of majesty which God undertook. I am personally very glad that the divine child was born in a stable, because my soul is very much like a stable, filled with strange unsatisfied longings, with guilt and animal-like impulses, tormented by anxiety, inadequacy and pain. If the holy One could be born in such a place, this One can be born in me also. I am not excluded.

Anyone who has studied the Bible with a critical eye knows that the events surrounding this birth are not as well documented as the later parts of our story. Mark does not speak of them, and John speaks of them in quite another way. Nonetheless the whole story hangs together and is made of the same cloth as Jesus' teachings, ministry, and death. For me it all fits together and it touches even the Scrooge in most of us at Christmas time. It is important to realize that the New Testament tradition started with the resurrection of Jesus and moved back through his death and ministry. This was the burning message. As years went by the importance of Jesus' human life began to be realized, and evangelists later added details of his birth from the womb of memory. Raymond Brown has provided an excellent scholarly analysis of the birth stories in his book, *The Birth of the Messiah*. His conclusion is much the same as mine—that there are few places in the entire Gospel story where the essence of Christian theology is presented with greater clarity and insight.[2]

The coming of the divine into the world could not be entirely hidden. It was too much of a good thing. Later when Jesus healed lepers and those possessed by demons, he usually told them to tell no one, but they could not keep quiet. When he entered Jerusalem on Palm Sunday and the crowds cried out, and covered his path with palms and clothes, he said that if they hadn't, the very stones would have raised their voices in welcome. This same welcome is seen in the birth narrative. As God broke into the world nature rejoiced in joyous sympathy and a star blazed out in the heavens. Nature could not keep still.

Wise men who watched the stars and read the message of nature in them saw that they spoke of a new king and a new kingdom. They set out over hot and barren deserts, through unfamiliar and hostile territories, over cold and snowy mountain passes. But they had not read the entire message of the stars, and before they came to lay their gifts before the child they went to Herod's palace to inquire about the new king—a first-class blunder. However these travelers remind us that even the intelligent and privileged can find the new life if they work hard enough at it.

The evil powers in the world worked through Herod, who was terrified by the news. A new king meant that his house would be displaced, and so he demanded that he be notified once they found the child. While the wise men continued their journey, there were shepherds, the poorest of the poor, in the fields watching their flocks. They were outcasts, the humblest of human beings, chilled to the bone as they huddled around their fires. It was only to them that the angel came to announce the peace which the birth could bring to humankind. They left their fires and came to pay homage to the One born in a stable. The child was circumcised and purified, and then the parents brought the child to the temple in Jerusalem. There the holy One was recognized by two people with inner vision who had been praying for the redemption of Israel.

In many medieval paintings of the birth of Jesus you will find a crucifix hanging half hidden on one of the rough beams of the stable. This symbolism has a powerful meaning: the entrance of the divine into the world resulted in strange and tragic consequences. The way of God was different from what humans would have thought. An angel warned the naïve magi in a dream that Herod's intentions left something to be desired, and they went home another way. Still, evil tried its best to destroy the beachhead of God in the world. Herod was furious and called in the military. Since he could not find *the* child, he sent his soldiers into Bethlehem to destroy all the male children under two. Joseph was warned in a dream and fled in the night over the wild sands to Egypt with Mary and the infant Jesus. Every approaching horse raised the specter of fear. Were the soldiers of Herod about to overtake them? Like so many in our world today the holy family were refugees in a hostile or at least indifferent land. And while they fled, the holy innocents were slaughtered in Bethlehem. Significantly, the Church remembers the death of Stephen, the first martyr, at the same time of the year.

The battle had begun, but evil was not able to snuff out the holy One. When Herod died, Joseph and Mary and their child returned to Nazareth and continued their hidden existence. Only once that we know of did the boy Jesus show his later promise. He stayed behind in Jerusalem in the temple asking questions of the religious leaders and listening to them. Then the curtain goes down and the disguise became complete.

How difficult it is for most of us to believe that God came into our world, that he was incarnated, was made flesh, took residence in physical creation. If, indeed, this physical world were simply illusion, it would be very simple for divine beings to rip apart the illusion and let their reality shine forth. The physical world is not redeemed by such an action; it is just an illusion temporarily set aside. It is quite another matter for the divine to take up residence in a physical world that is real. Then nature cannot be evil or ugly in itself, for it is good enough to carry the very fullness of divinity.

On the other hand, if we believe in the reality of the physical world but believe that there is no spiritual world, or that if one exists we human beings can know nothing about it, then the idea of this invasion of God is ridiculous and impossible. However, there is still another view of reality that has been held by many people in different ages and times. In this view there are two dimensions of reality, and a God who created them both. They are both potentially good even though evil has broken out in both of them. These worlds are interlocking and the spiritual penetrates the physical, yet has an existence of its own apart from the physical. In particular, the spirit of God has a foothold within the depth of each human psyche. If this is the case, it is not surprising that God could enter totally into a human soul and so unite with a human body and become flesh.

I find two diagrams or models helpful at this point. In the first is sketched the whole universe—the physical world, the spiritual world surrounding it on all sides, human beings caught between these two and a bridge between them, the reality of God and the reality of evil and the many spiritual realities and contents in both worlds. The triangle is an image of the human being, participating in two realities, two modes of existence. Through sense experience and ego consciousness we are able to reach out into the limited physical world (represented by the box in the center) and learn how to deal with it. Humans come to experience more and more of this world; it is sometimes ecstatically beautiful and good and at other times filled with horror and evil. We can also turn inward and find the same good and evil within us. We can also find that good and evil are not just human properties; they have an independent spiritual reality outside of us. The human triangle is limited and defined. Evil is also limited, but the Creator God is represented by the open parabola which expands infinitely. This God has placed the imprint of the divine image and reality within the human soul; this imprint, represented by the area where the parabola overlaps the triangle, is the human spirit.

This diagram presents the same data as the picture of the human beings between the two great ranges of mountains which we suggested in an earlier chapter. In the universe depicted in this first picture, we may believe that God is more powerful than evil, but we have no conclusive evidence for this faith. Creation is at loose ends and incomplete. In the spiritual domain God may have incredible power, but evil seems to have its own well-established place in the physical world which is so much with us.

In the second diagram the divine reality totally overshadows and penetrates the nature of a unique human being, and becomes united with the psyche of Jesus of Nazareth. Through this person God becomes flesh and has concrete physical access to the divinely created world. This is incarnation, God entering into the nature that God created. This is one of the greatest mysteries of all times. The Church struggled with the problem for centuries and came to the conclusion in the creed of Chalcedon that Jesus, the Christ, was perfect man and total God at the same time, fully human and fully divine without the two being mixed and mingled. This incredible paradox was one of the most important statements of the undivided Church.

The intense presence of the divine reality in the person of Jesus effectively prevented evil from being present within Jesus.

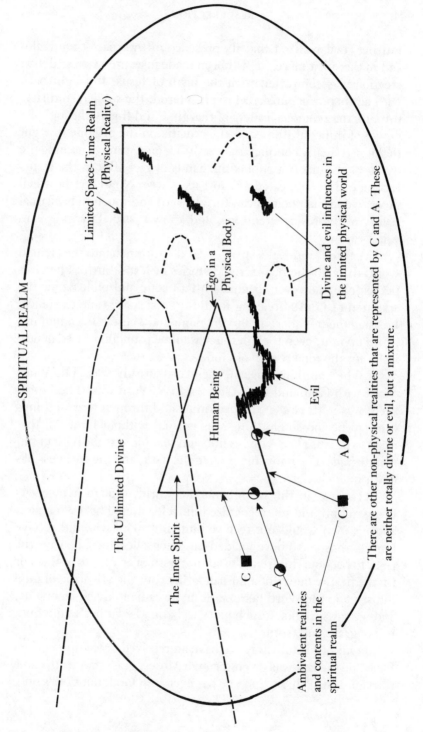

SPIRITUAL REALM

Limited Space-Time Realm
(Physical Reality)

Divine and evil influences in
the limited physical world

Ego in a
Physical Body

Human Being

Evil

The Unlimited Divine

The Inner Spirit

Ambivalent realities
and contents in the
spiritual realm

There are other non-physical realities that are represented by C and A. These
are neither totally divine or evil, but a mixture.

57

Further, evil realized that its presence in the space-time realm and in the spiritual realm had been made insecure because divine creation was completed with the birth of Jesus. It fought back with all its power through Joseph, Herod, the soldiers and later through the religious leaders of that time and finally through the power of imperial Rome. At the crucifixion the evil one thought that it had finally conquered, and sitting on a stump watching the dying God-human it rubbed its hands in glee. But in the resurrection evil was defeated and lost its power. No matter how evil rages, we human beings can turn inward and touch the spiritual reality of the resurrected One, and know that evil's raging is in vain.

Matthew and Luke speak of God's entrance into the created world through the pictures and stories of Jesus' birth. The Gospel of John, however, begins with a poetic and philosophic description of God's breaking forth into our space-time existence. His statement is short and to the point and I certainly cannot improve upon it, even though the masculine pronoun is used generically for the total reality of God.

"When all things began, the Word already was. The Word dwelt with God, and what God was, the Word was. The Word, then, was with God at the beginning and through him all things came to be; no single thing was created without him. All that came to be was alive with his life, and that life was the light of human beings. The light shines on in the dark, and the darkness has never quenched it. . . .

"He was in the world, but the world, though it owed its being to him, did not recognize him. He entered his own realm, and his own would not receive him. But to all who did receive him, to those who have yielded him their allegiance, he gave the right to become children of God, not born of any human stock, or by the fleshly desire of a human father, but the offspring of God himself. So the Word became flesh; he came to dwell among us, and we saw his glory, such glory as befits the Father's only Son, full of grace and truth. . . .

"Out of his full store we have all received grace upon grace; for while the law was given through Moses, grace and truth came through Jesus Christ. No one has ever seen God; but God's only

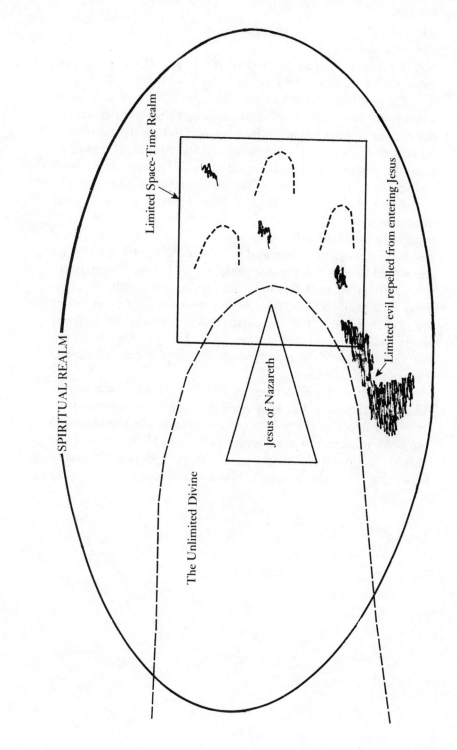

SPIRITUAL REALM

Limited Space-Time Realm

Limited evil repelled from entering Jesus

Jesus of Nazareth

The Unlimited Divine

Son, he who is nearest to the Father's heart, he has made him known" (NEB altered, Jn 1:1–5, 10–14, 16–18).

The coming of God in the flesh brought a new level of wholeness to creation. Until this happened the next two acts of our play were impossible. In incarnation God moved personally into the drama so that human beings could be rescued, ransomed from the power of evil and given a glorious heritage. God came and showed forth the nature of the divine in the fabric of time, in Palestine in the reign of Tiberius Caesar. Evil did its best to snuff out this rescuing light. Had our story ended with the baby in the manger or the child in Egypt or even with the remarkable young man talking with the priests and learned leaders of the temple, no one would be much interested in the story. It is necessary to remember once again at this point that it was not simply the coming of God as a baby in a stable which made the difference; rather it was what flowed out of this event, this person who grew up and taught and lived and *died and rose again*. On the other hand the true significance of the next five acts of our play depends on the truth of the incarnation.

Incarnation is the sowing of the divine seed in the world. What was the plant like that grew from this sowing? God revealed the depth of the holy center of all reality in the historical Jesus. What image of God emerges as the inner being of God unfolds in the life and teachings, in the actions of Jesus of Nazareth? This brings us to the next act of the divine drama.

5.

God Present in the World: The Historical and Human Jesus of Nazareth

Without warning or preparation Jesus of Nazareth suddenly blazed forth on the historical scene. Three of the Gospel writers simply state that Jesus first came into view as a national figure in the time of John the Baptist. The account of the contemporary Jewish historian Josephus describes the ministry and death of John the Baptist in much the same manner as we find depicted in the Gospel narratives. Luke was much more specific. He was interested that we see both John and Jesus in the context of history. The events he was about to describe were so extraordinary that he wanted to make sure they were not considered just mythology. He wrote: "In the fifteenth year of the Emperor Tiberius, when Pontius Pilate was governor of Judea, when Herod was prince of Galilee, his brother Philip prince of Iturea and Trachonitis, and Lysanias prince of Abilene, during the high priesthood of Annas and Caiaphas, the word of God came to John, son of Zechariah in the wilderness" (3:1–3). He preached repentance for the forgiveness of sins and baptized multitudes who came to him for this ceremonial cleansing.

Jesus of Nazareth came to the Jordan River to be baptized by John. According to Luke he was thirty years old. As he prayed following the baptism, the realization of his unique person and destiny broke in upon him in a new way. He came to his God-consciousness and went off into the wilderness to wrestle through the insights and experiences that came to him. The devil

61

was ready and came to tempt him with political, social and religious power, but Jesus remained loyal to the God of love, to his own inner being. The attack of evil that he experienced there in the wild desert was to continue in one form or another throughout his ministry. Jung comments on the temptation narrative: if Jesus had projected the devil out into the outer world there would have been "one madman the more in the world." Instead Jesus dealt with this experience as something from the spiritual world and so "entered the world as a king, unto whom the kingdoms of heaven *are* subject." Jung goes on to say: "The views advanced from time to time from the psychiatric side concerning the morbidity of Christ's psychology are nothing but ludicrous rationalistic twaddle with no comprehension whatever of the meaning of such processes in the history of mankind."[1]

Around one hundred years ago some students of the New Testament, reacting against the dogmatism of the Church and in the first flush of a critical study of the Bible, suggested that Jesus was not even a real historical figure. Using the same arguments put forward by these writers someone "proved" that the historicity of Julius Caesar could also be doubted. Forty years ago some biblical critics were teaching dogmatically that the Gospels tell us more about the early Christian community than about the historical Jesus. Recent scholarship expressed in Gunther Bornkamm's *Jesus of Nazareth* comes to a more reasonable point of view. Certainly we do not have a modern biography of Jesus in the Gospels, and some of the stories and sayings of Jesus have been colored by the concerns of the early Church. However, we still have an amazingly accurate historical picture of this striking man and his ministry.[2] I know of no better picture of the historical and human Jesus of Nazareth than Andrew Canale's recent book, *Understanding the Human Jesus*. Dr. Canale presents an accurate and detailed picture of this incredible human being with a depth of psychological understanding and in the context of a genuine personal response.

In addition to the historical material provided by the Gospels we have the New Testament letters. Some of these are considered coming from the hand of Paul by nearly every serious scholar, and they were written no more than fifteen years subsequent to Jesus' resurrection. Ongoing archeological research has supported the geographical and historical accuracy of Luke's Acts of the Apostles. There are few more detailed accounts of navigating through a storm in the first century than the one found in Acts. I was amazed to find in my visits to Palestine the remains of early Christian churches at the places significant in the life of Jesus. Some of these date back to late apostolic times. The startling contention of Christianity is that the divine invaded the world to show the nature of God to humankind in the person and being of Jesus of Nazareth. As we begin to look at Jesus' life in greater depth we shall necessarily look again at some of the events we have already discussed; but now we look at these events from a new perspective.

The Ministry

As Jesus returned from his confrontation with the evil one in the wilderness, he set out to proclaim the good news: "The time has been fulfilled and the Kingdom of God has drawn near; repent and believe the glad tidings." He gathered a group of followers around him, an intimate group of twelve men who lived with him and shared his life and ministry. Jesus evidently knew the value of group process in teaching. By any standard Jesus was unusual for his time. Not only did he gather this group of men, but he valued women and children and welcomed some women into his entourage. He spoke as a prophet directly in contact with God. He could use the rabbinical method when discoursing on a text, but he also spoke with authority. He ministered to the poor and the outcast, often viewed by the religious authorities as objects of God's disfavor; he entered the questionable ranks of those who healed the sick, the mentally ill and the demon-possessed; he turned over the ideas about wealth being a sign of God's favor; he taught new ways of prayer and gave sacramental rites to be performed; he spoke of the utter centrality of love as the key to understanding the nature of God. And he was an incarnation of that love.

At first the ministry of Jesus drew great crowds. The Jewish nation was seething, and many people saw Jesus as the hoped for political leader who would bring freedom from the Romans. As the true nature of his message became better understood, the throngs dwindled. But the religious leaders realized that he still posed a threat to their power, security and privilege and they became increasingly hostile. After a ministry that lasted from two to three years, Jesus came up to the Holy City and there confronted the religious and political authorities. He was condemned by the religious leaders of his own people, turned over to the Romans, and crucified.

Hundreds of books have been written on nearly every aspect of Jesus' life and ministry. It is almost foolish to summarize, but I believe that we can see a central movement in the pattern of his life. Jesus expresses his own and God's unfathomable love for human beings—broken, disfigured, hostile, destructive, proud, hateful, greedy, corrupt and rebellious as all of us are. He shows this in his teaching of the ultimate value of each concrete human being, in his directions on praying and ritual, in his healing ministry, in his revelation of the love of God, and finally by his courage as he confronted the evil one and walked calmly and decisively into torture and an agonizing death.

Probably no one in history has had more influence upon human morality and ethical thinking. Not only did Jesus consider each human soul to be of infinite and irreplaceable value; he felt that the concrete, outer physical condition of each human was of infinite importance to God. God has no favorites. No one human being should suffer or be liquidated for the good of other human beings. No one is expendable. The message of his birth in a stable is reinforced in everything he said. The beggars in spirit (a more accurate translation of the Greek of the first Beatitude than the usual one) are to be given the Kingdom of heaven. We do not have to become gurus to be acceptable.

What he did was the same as what he said. He welcomed a tax collector (considered a traitor by most Jews) into his inner circle. He told the story of the Samaritan and the man who fell among thieves in order to clarify the meaning of the word neighbor. He expanded the Old Testament understanding of that term to include even the despised Samaritan who, if anything, was in a lower category than the tax collector and the prostitute. He contrasted the compassion of the outcast Samaritan with the religious leader's fear of ritual impurity. In his story the respected rich man who does not care for the beggar at his gate is deprived of heaven. And yet he purposely sought out the wealthy Zacchaeus because he perceived compassion in him. Compassion, for Jesus, is more important than status in life, almost more important than anything else. He ministered to the poor from among whose number he came. He condemned only one group of people, the religious leaders of his people who covered the practice of religion with so many rules that ordinary poor people could not follow them. He felt that these leaders were lacking in compassion because they were denying God's people access to the boundless love of God, that love which could make their lives whole and joyful now as well as in the world to come. No class or group of people was to be rejected or despised, not the rich nor the poor, not the pagan, the Jew nor the Samaritan, not the prostitute nor the quisling, the leper nor the mentally diseased. But those in any group who could not forgive and show compassion were in danger of totally missing the mark.

So striking was the message and ministry of love in Jesus that many readers and even students of the Gospels have placed Jesus in the wrong category. They have seen him as a detached, Greek ethical teacher so common in the first century when in fact Jesus was filled with a mysterious power. Not only did he preach, but as an instrument of that love he healed the sick and broken and demon-possessed. He was a shaman as well as a moralist. How difficult it has been for Western men and women during the last two centuries to understand this aspect of Jesus' ministry. The people of third world nations who are closer to nature have less trouble understanding Jesus' ministry of power.

It is truly amazing what we can avoid in a total picture when it does not fit with our pre-conceptions and basic understanding of the world. More pages of the Gospel narrative are devoted to the healings of Jesus than to moral instruction. In a world that viewed the sick as tainted and as suffering divine displeasure, Jesus' healings offer quite a different view of the nature of God. This is not the place to go into all the evidence for the significance of healing in Jesus' ministry, in the practice of the apostles and the early Church, and among the saints from that time to this. In

my book *Healing and Christianity*, I deal in depth with this neglected part of Jesus' ministry and the reasons for the neglect. My
Benedictine friend, Jean Leclercq, read this study of mine and remarked that he had seldom seen a better description of the love of
Jesus and of God than in these acts of compassion to the sick, suffering and sorrowing. It was almost as if God incarnate in human
flesh could not abide what disfigured the divine image within human beings. From a tactical point of view it might have been better not to call attention to himself, and he warned most of those
healed not to speak of their restoration, but it appears as if he
could not withhold his healing love. Jesus was opposed to the
forces of evil that caused sickness, and his compassion went out
to those whom evil had damaged.

The early Church Fathers believed that the evil one whom
they personified as *Death* attacks human beings, inducing them to
sin, causing mental illness, physical disease and finally death. Jesus, as the incarnation of life, was set against these ravages of
Death. Those who doubt the importance of faith to open us to
transforming power have read little of the observable power of
faith healers, psychologists, shamans, and holy places. The actual healings at Lourdes are quite astounding. The appreciation
of the creative power available (and all creative power is ultimately of God) in sacramental touch and action is growing on
every side. These transformations can be wrought through our
own faith or through the faith of others. To have the power to as-
suage human misery and pain and not to do so is not even human,
let alone divine.

When his disciples asked Jesus to teach them to pray, he
gave them the prayer known to us all. We are so used to it that we
don't see how startling and radical it is. Most of the time we are
dragging God down to our level. Jesus tells us that any of us can
turn to Abba, the mother-father God. Indeed the word Abba is
better translated as mommy-daddy, the familiar term small children use to call out to a caring, loving parent. Abba wishes our
presence even when we are ugly, deformed, nasty, destructive,
fearful and sinning human beings. One of Jesus' basic beliefs was
that we can make direct and open contact with this loving One.
We don't have to use long formulas or repetitions. We ask that
God's holiness may shine forth, that the Kingdom of heaven may

come within us and around us, and that we may be able to do God's will. In the Greek the imperative is used; we command that the Kingdom come. We ask for our human, earthly needs and for the needs of every other person in the world, which necessitates our getting involved in social action to help these others, and then we ask to be forgiven and to be helped to forgive. Finally we ask because of our weakness not to be put to the test and also to be protected and delivered from the evil one, for we cannot defeat this power by ourselves. For thirty years I have been using this prayer as a framework of praying and find it inexhaustible in depth and fruitfulness. Sometimes I need twenty minutes of quiet to center into it, and praying it can take half an hour.

By his own baptism Jesus sanctified a sacrament of initiation. What was so valuable to him certainly will be as valuable to us. His attendance at the synagogue services and his journeys to Jerusalem for the great festivals showed how much he valued the communal aspect of prayer and religion. Jesus and his intimate friends often ate together, and those meals had great significance. The feeding of the multitudes speaks of a sacramental aspect of eating. It was, however, the final passover meal he shared with his disciples before his betrayal and death which struck home to his followers. They sensed that this meal was a place where they could meet him again.

Two of the most striking resurrection encounters were connected with a shared meal: the stories of the two travelers at Emmaus and the disciples at the Sea of Galilee. Many people throughout the ages have experienced meeting their risen Lord in a unique way in the breaking of the bread and the sharing of the cup. Indeed the Eucharist has been the normative communal Christian form of prayer throughout the breadth of most of the Church in all ages. Jesus has provided for both our inner private communion with Abba and also for our experience of Abba in our common worship together. And then there is the forgotten sacrament, the footwashing. According to John, Jesus commanded his followers to wash one another's feet; he told them to follow his almost unbelievable example. How Jesus turned things upside down! How seldom gurus wash novices' feet!

In his parables and stories Jesus described the nature of God

and the Kingdom of heaven so clearly and graphically that anyone could understand what he was saying. In *The Kingdom Within*
John Sanford has shown the extraordinary depth and wisdom in
some of these parables. The stories that Jesus told and the story
he lived both spoke the same integral message and an astounding
one at that. Again our eyes are blinded by familiarity. A student
at the University of Notre Dame awakened me afresh to the startling and surprising nature of Jesus' life and message. He was a
brilliant young man consumed by darkness and despair. In order
to offer hope to him I suggested that he read the New Testament
as if it were a novel. He was a conventional church member and
had never read it before. I will never forget how different he
looked during our next meeting and how he burst out: "This
man, Jesus, was a freak-out." It was one of the highest and most
genuine appreciations of Jesus that I have ever heard.

The Gospel Within the Gospel

    Probably no tale of this master story-teller expressed more
of the essence of Jesus' message than the engaging story of the
man with two sons. Popularly known as the parable of the prodigal son, this parable speaks more centrally about the extravagant
love of the prodigal father than of the son's escapades. This story
has been called the gospel within the Gospel. Let us take this
story as our guide to Jesus' central meaning. As we examine it in
depth we will begin to see how radical, revolutionary and overwhelming this message really is.
    Try to imagine yourself one of a crowd of Jews listening to
Jesus as he told about the prosperous farmer with two sons. If
this account appears absurd to us, how much more so it appeared
to those who first heard it. The younger son was probably about
seventeen when he made his startling request: "Life is dull here
on the ranch and I want to live, live, live. Soon the best years of
my life will be gone. Please give me now the share of my property
which is due me as my inheritance and let me go." Few parents
would be surprised by such a request in our day, but it was unthinkable in the society of Jesus' time. Children just did not speak

to their parents that way. In addition, the son was inferring (not too subtly) that he wished his father dead.

Jesus' listeners were aghast, but this was nothing compared to what came next. The father listened quietly, embraced his son and said: "You can have your share in seven days. We will make an accounting for you." Meanwhile the servants who were on the other side of the thin partitions looked at one another in unbelief. What had happened to the master? When the elder brother was informed he secretly wondered if his father had lost his wits. Nothing remains secret in a small village, and everyone knew that the younger son was about to turn his property into cash and go off to the big city. When he came into the village to turn his inheritance into gold, the merchants were ready for him and they offered him hardly half what his goods and chattel were worth, but he was seventeen and impatient and took what he could get. How those listening to the story would have laughed at the stupidity of this absurd son and father.

The younger son set out immediately. I am sure that he headed for Antioch. No Jewish city was open enough. Antioch was known as the cesspool of the ancient world. About this time Rome became corrupt, and one Roman writer of the old school lamented that the Orontes (the river which flowed through Antioch) had begun to flow into mother Tiber, the river of Rome. And where did our young man go when he arrived in Antioch? Undoubtedly he sought out a Roman bath. Decency forbids that I describe in any detail what went on in a Roman bath. Suffice it to say that it was a pornographic bookstore in 3-D. The younger son had his supply of gold, solid currency in that age as well as in our own; with it he began his riotous and reckless living filled with wine, women and song. How long his money lasted, how long this lifestyle went on, we cannot tell. But inevitably the time came when his money was gone and those who had shared the grasshopper summer with him laughed at his entreaties for help and would have nothing to do with him. At the same time one of the often recurring famines struck the land. This brash young fellow with no skill but enthusiasm could find no work. He sold all the treasures he had accumulated, and when these were gone, he began to get hungrier and hungrier. At last in order to survive he hired out to a Gentile swine herder to tend pigs.

Again we need to place ourselves in the shoes of the Jews who first heard this story to appreciate the full significance of this detail. The youth had already broken the moral law in his riotous living, but the Jewish religious tradition was remarkably realistic about human weakness in sexual matters; also overindulgence in food and drink in an economy of scarcity was considered quite leniently. Proverbs warned against prostitutes, but on the other hand prostitutes were common, and at least one prostitute, Rahab, was a national heroine. Jesus' listeners would have agreed that the younger son was certainly off base in what he did, but after all he got what was coming to him.

The tending and feeding of pigs was quite another matter. This was a flagrant violation of ritual law and custom. It was forbidden in the law to eat pork, to touch the carcass of a pig or to offer swine's blood as a sacrifice.[3] In the Talmud, a later elaboration of the Jewish law, the pig was the very symbol of ritual uncleanness, and those who tended them were treated with aversion bordering on disgust. This attitude shaped the reactions of those to whom Jesus spoke. A gasp of horror rose from the crowd as Jesus shared this detail of this story. The prodigal had not only broken the moral law, but had utterly defiled himself as if he had been bathing in a cesspool. The only comparable horror that we can understand is the attitude toward adultery and fornication in Boston in 1700.

Finally the broken young man came to himself, but I have never been much impressed with his conversion. His stomach pinched. When he came to himself he did not consider his father's love and mercy and return for these. He only wanted to fill his stomach and reasoned that his father's servants had enough and more to eat, and here he was starving and longing to eat the food the pigs were eating. He thought to himself: "It is better to live than to die. I will set out toward home and I will tell my father: 'Father, I have sinned, against God and against you; I am no longer fit to be called your son; treat me as one of your servants.' " Almost immediately he started on his homeward trek.

During this period the father received no news of his wayward son. His heart was heavy and aching. Each morning he would go out to a hill on the edge of his property, hoping to see his son returning. There he could look over the whole countryside. Again he went in the late afternoon. One day after many, many months on a far-off hill he saw a dark speck, a human figure. Anyone who thinks that love is blind has never loved. Even at that distance the father knew it was his lost child. How true are Laurens Van der Post's words: "If there is one thing that love is not, it is blind. If it possesses a blindness at all, it is a blindness to the man and the man-made blindnesses of life; to the dead-ends, the cul-de-sacs and hopelessnesses of our being. In all else it is clear and far-sighted as the sun. When the world and judgment say: 'This is the end,' love alone can see the way out. It is the aboriginal tracker, the African bushman on the faded desert spoor within us, and its unfailing quarry is always the light."[4]

In his book *The Cross and the Prodigal* Kenneth Bailey points out the radical quality of the Greek words describing the meeting of the son and his father.[5] First of all the father raced toward this son as soon as he recognized him. The word used in Greek is the same one used to describe running a footrace in Greek athletic games. A semitic man of the father's age walked with dignity, and the father certainly had not raced anywhere in many years. In order to run he must either tuck his long robe into his girdle or take it in his hand. And then (shamefully) his underwear might show. When the father started to run, his servants and any other villagers around knew that something of immense importance was about to take place. When the father reached his son he flung his arms around his son and held him to his bosom and kissed him again and again with compassionate care.

The son hardly knew what was happening as he was gathered into the father's arms. He stammered out his well-prepared little speech, but never even finished it. His father cut him off and began to give orders to his servants who had followed and stood awestruck. He called for three gifts of incredible significance: a robe, a ring and shoes. A tradition of long standing among biblical critics has stated dogmatically that parables can only have one central meaning, and most commentators follow this tradition without thinking. In *Transforming Bible Study* Walter Wink has pointed out clearly that each part of a parable can be a symbol of unfathomable meaning just as each image of a dream can lead deep into mystery. One of the reasons Jesus speaks to the depth of the human heart as much today as ever is that he not only engages our rational thinking side, but he also speaks in the universal language of symbols. Through the same type of imagery the depths of the soul speak in dreams.[6]

First of all Bailey reminds us that the father does not say: "Now go home and take a shower and shave and get some decent clothes on and then we will talk." Rather he dispatches his servants to get a robe, the best one, and he dresses him up just as he himself is, in regal attire. The father plans a great feast because this his son was dead and is alive again; he was lost and is found. There will be guests. It is not easy to be a prodigal returning home. The old family friends come up and ask: "And where have you been?" The father was trying to stave off as much of this embarrassment as possible. In addition I get the impression of a certain impatience in the father. He wanted the son's image restored immediately so that the son might begin to change his own self-image. How important clothes are in the modern business world; they are one key to business success and social acceptance. In dreams they represent the face we show to the world, our persona as Jung calls it. Jesus told another story about a person who came to the wedding feast without a wedding garment, unprepared, without the right attitude. The father knows that this image has to change before the son can allow himself to be received. The new image is given by the father as pure, free gift. Imagine how relieved the son was to be stripped of his old, torn, foul-smelling dirty clothes. The gift of the robe was an act of compassion in many different ways and on many different levels.

The servants were also directed to hurry back home and get a ruby signet ring and place it on his finger. The youth needed the shoes and the robe, but was not the gift of a ring overdoing it a bit? Why that ring? The Greek is very clear. Such a ring was far more than an ornament, although it was that too. This ring gave the returned wastrel legal authority in the family. Such a ring was used to sign a contract or a will. Even today such a ring is used by villagers in the Near East to sign official documents. He had wasted the family fortune and was now legally integrated back into the family fortune. No wonder the elder brother was furious. And then there was the deep symbolism of the ring as a sign of relationship. For how many centuries has the ring been used as a symbol of the union of marriage? What incredible forgiveness! How utterly unjust from one point of view! This story, however, is not of justice, but of more than justice, of full-throated, unbounded gracious mercy.

And then the shoes. The boy needed the shoes, no doubt. His feet were torn and bleeding. His own shoes had long ago worn out and fallen apart. He had traveled the long distance home over rough roads in bare feet. His feet were not hardened to such conditions. Slaves and bond-servants did not wear shoes in the ancient world. Their feet developed thick calluses, rough and hard, but the prodigal was the son of a householder and had been brought up in shoes. The gift of shoes snatched him right out of the class of servant and made him a son again. This gift was mercy on several levels. Shoes are also a recurrent symbol in dreams today and signify our standpoint, our basic stance, our view of reality. A new view of himself and those around him was given to the son. Seldom do we achieve this by ourselves. It is given.

Slowly father and son, servants and the growing crowd wound their way back toward the father's house. The father ordered the fatted calf to be slaughtered and prepared for the feast. Any kind of meat was a delicacy in that world, but this was the choicest prime meat. A class of children was studying this story, and after hearing the entire story the teacher asked them: "Whom do you feel most sorry for?" One little girl spoke up with a sob in her voice: "The fatted calf."

And this brings us to the elder son, the workaholic over-achiever who was out in the field managing the family affairs. It had been a long, hot, hard day; the sun had set and he was tired. As he rounded the bend he heard music and saw the flicker of many torches. He wondered what the addled old man was up to now. He had a servant boy with him and sent him to run ahead and find out what on earth was going on there. The boy returned wide-eyed and amazed and poured out the news. He had never seen such a party before. "Your brother has returned and your father has prepared a great feast and invited everyone because he has received him safe and sound." At this the faithful and right-eous son blew up. He may have even cuffed the servant. He then sent the boy back into the party to the father with these words: "I won't come to your stupid feast." How difficult it is for the righteous to have mercy. After all, the younger son had had his share of the property. The party was coming out of the elder son's inheritance!

The refusal of this elder son to come to the party was in many ways a far greater breach of semitic morality, manners and etiquette than the wildness of the prodigal. It was defiance and rejection of the father and his values. The prodigal had been a fool and had returned home, and even in that society it was possible to imagine him being grafted back into the family, though perhaps not with the lavish extravagance of the story. The older son threw over his father's authority and rebuked him for what he had done. In a sense he killed his father. He was totally out of place. How could one reach out to such defiance without losing face? Much of the trouble in the Near East today results from refusal to lose face. Going out to the elder brother in some ways was a greater act of mercy, more a breaking of the customary than the reception given the prodigal. The parent expects to be obeyed, not to go out to the young and plead with them. But this father goes the second mile.

Not only is the young fool received and loved, but the arrogant, unforgiving and defiant son is sought out. Hurt and angry, the faithful son launches into a tirade against his father (again quite unthinkable in that society): "You know how I have slaved for you all these years; I have never once disobeyed your orders; you never gave me so much as a young goat to make merry with my friends. But now *this son of yours* turns up, after running through your money and property with prostitutes, and you kill for him the calf we have been fattening." And still the father reaches out and pleads. His is a security that defiance does not threaten.

Jesus was a good story teller and so his tale breaks off at this point. What happened? I believe that the elder brother finally softened and came reluctantly to the feast, and there ate and drank. And over the weeks that came and went perhaps he even allowed the love and mercy of the father to penetrate him.

What is the point of this story? The message is ridiculously clear. This story is set between the stories of the woman searching for the lost coin and the shepherd seeking his lost sheep on the one side and the story of the unjust steward on the other—all stories of the unfathomable, unrelenting, ever-present, inhuman, merciful love of God. Jesus says to us that God is like a shepherd seeking a lost lamb on a dark night or a woman seeking her lost coin or a master forgiving a steward who has swindled the master's goods. Jesus was telling those who listened to him: "God is like that prodigal father. God is not what you think. God receives prodigals and goes out to stuffy elder brothers. God loves and wants to gather all of us into the Kingdom now and forever."

Such a message is very difficult for us to take seriously. Why should we believe that God is like that? How many of us have ever been treated like that when we returned home after messing up our lives? How many of us have been lovingly entreated to be kind when we have been self-righteous and scornful of love? The more that we are treated with this kind of love by parents and other significant people around us, the easier it becomes for us to believe the message of Jesus about God. The real reason for the Church is to provide us a fellowship of this kind in which we can practice the merciful life of the Kingdom in the here and now. Tragically, however, the Church is often the last place where prodigals feel free to return or where the defiant faithful are entreated with tender understanding.

I doubt if I could take the story Jesus told very seriously if I did not know the story that he lived. Again and again I think of two statues in the great chapel of Notre Dame. On one side of the high altar in this church in the very center of the University of Notre Dame is a magnificent bronze statue by Ivan Mestrovic of the prodigal returned, with his head buried in his father's arms. On the other side of the altar is a monumental marble of the Pieta by the same sculptor, with Joseph of Arimathea standing behind Mary, who is holding the body of her son. One is the story Jesus told, the other the story that he lived.

The Cross

The story Jesus enacted in real life is even more radical than the one he told. In the historical story the prodigal did not return

home, but Jesus died for all the lost even before they came to
themselves. It was as if the father found him lying in a foul prison
and condemned to death. The son can be released only if someone is willing to die for him. The father gives himself up for the
son and is tortured and hung on a cross. All this takes place before the younger son has come to himself or the elder brother has
softened.

As we read the story of those last days of Jesus we find variations among the various accounts of the events, and as we look
at the resurrection we will discover the same variety. Some people are bothered by this, but I am happy that we perceive these
events through different eyes and ears. If all the descriptions
were identical I would believe that they had been cut down to
size and harmonized. Like true eyewitnesses, those who describe
the events are struck by different aspects of the drama they lived
through. A forgery of a signature can often be detected because it
will be identical to one other example of the person's handwrit-
ing. But no two genuine signatures are identical. Similarly, no
two reactions to a drama or to history are identical.

Near the end of his ministry Jesus set his face toward Jerusalem to go up for the Passover feast. He had warned his disciples
that his messiahship, his kingship, his Kingdom was different
from what they thought. He predicted his own suffering and
death. He knew what was before him when he started back to the
Holy City. Mark tells that his followers saw something uncanny
in his presence as he started this last journey. They camped outside the city near the Garden of Gethsemane during the festival
as the city swarmed with Jews from all over the Roman world.
On the first day of the week he entered the great city riding on a
donkey. A great multitude gathered. Jesus was entering as king
of peace, and he did not come unannounced and secretly. He
flung down the gauntlet to his people, to the Romans, to the
world, to the evil one. In the days that followed, Jesus and his followers came into the city daily. Evil tried every ploy to discredit
him. There were conflicts with the religious authorities. They
tried to trap him, but he responded with great depth and wisdom. The final straw for them was undoubtedly his cleansing of
the temple, the sacred center of the Jewish religion and cultural
life. There he drove out the money changers and those who

bought and sold. He cried out that this place was meant to be a house of prayer and that it had become a den of thieves.

Evil, acting through the fear of the religious leaders, decided that it was better that one man die than that the nation be destroyed. One of his disciples plotted with them to betray him. Perhaps Judas was disillusioned, or trying to force Jesus' hand; or perhaps he acted from a mixture of motives that even he did not understand. Jesus gathered his disciples together for one last meal, this time a passover meal. John writes that Jesus played the part of the lowest kind of servant and washed their feet. He told them that one of them would betray him and that they would all desert him. They all cried out their denials, and then Judas went out and it was night. Singing psalms, the rest of the band went out to the garden and there Jesus went apart and prayed that this cup, this fate, might be taken from him. He asked some of the disciples to watch with him, but they were tired and slept. And then Judas arrived leading a band of the temple guard and signaled the right man to arrest by embracing and kissing Jesus. One of the disciples heard him say to Judas: "Friend, would you betray the Son of Man with a kiss?" Even in this extremity he spoke like the prodigal father.

The torture to which human beings subject each other is one of the best examples of evil possessing the human heart, and it is still common in our own day. Jesus was tormented first by the court of his own religious leaders. He was mocked, struck and condemned to death. To carry out the sentence they sent him on to the Roman governor because execution was Rome's sole prerogative.

Most of his closest friends fled after he was seized, but Peter, the rock, followed and denied him three times before the cock crowed twice just as Jesus had predicted. Some say that Jesus was taken before Herod Antipas. Finally Jesus was brought before Pilate and there condemned to die. According to Roman custom he was flogged (as if crucifixion were not enough) and then mocked by the soldiers, burdened with his own cross and taken out to be nailed on the cross to die.

Upon the cross he was reported to have spoken seven times. No wonder that he cried out in his utter humanity: "My God, my God, why have you forsaken me?" Suffering from traumatic thirst he called out from the depth of human physical suffering: "I thirst." To the penitent thief crucified with him he gave the consoling message: "Today you will be with me in paradise." To all those present and to all of us throughout the centuries he spoke: "Father, forgive them, for they know not what they do." Then to Mary and the beloved disciple, both standing by the cross, he spoke: "Mother, behold your son. Son, behold your mother." John took Mary under his care and protection from that hour. And as the sky darkened and nature shook in sympathy Jesus spoke twice again. First he said: "It is finished"—meaning that what he came for was completed. And then he uttered a loud cry and murmured: "Father, into your hands I commend my spirit." With these words Jesus of Nazareth died. A Gentile centurion standing beneath the cross knew that something incredible had happened and said: "Truly this man was the son of God."

Joseph of Arimathea obtained permission and came and took the body down together with Jesus' friends who lingered there. They carried the body to a new tomb belonging to Joseph. They had to hurry, because the sinking of the sun marked the beginning of the sabbath. They wrapped the body in a shroud and together rolled a great stone before the entrance to the tomb. Jesus' career was finished and done.

It was truly a remarkable death. Jesus' crucifixion tells us so much about evil and God. Jesus' death on that wood reveals the power of naked evil struggling to destroy our souls. More dangerous for most of us is the subtle evil of those who contributed to the crucifixion and did not even know it—the soldiers, the carpenter who made the cross, the crowd who were not there to cry out for Jesus, the righteous religious leaders trying to protect their nation, the tormented souls who came to watch this execution to forget their own misery. Nothing reveals the utter and total humanity of Jesus more clearly than the cross. He suffered and died like all those in torture chambers all over the world today. The events leading up to the crucifixion as well as the actual nailing and dying show the marvelous courage of this man and sanctify courage as one of the greatest of human virtues. Most important for me is the incomparable love which Jesus showed as he died for me and for others like me who could not survive without that sacrificial love. The darkness overwhelmed Jesus on the cross and then it passed. Even in his agony Jesus still had moments of hope on the cross. Part of him had faith that all this suffering was not in vain.

Crucifixion and death, however, were not what transformed the broken, frightened disciples and friends. They were hiding for fear that they would be sought out and crucified. Most of them had not had the courage to stay with him when he died. If agonized death were the end of the sad tale, then evil finally did conquer: God, goodness, love, kindness, mercy, peace and joy were in the end defeated and became will-o'-the-wisps. Brutality, power, murder, hatred, selfishness, bitterness and death are the bottom line, and Christians, as Paul reminded us in one of his letters, are the most ridiculous, stupid, unfortunate and deluded of all people—simple, sentimental unrealistic fools.

The cross stands at the fork of the road. It tells us to make a decision between two ways. It forces a decision from us. We can go down the meaningless road and follow one of two ways of traveling. We can try to be noble in the power of our own strength. Or we can race down that road with the power of evil and pry from life the best we can and then die laughing or crying. Sartre and many materialists tell us that there is no fork. There is only this one road. If there were no resurrection, these pessimists would be right. The cross can be the most tragic event of human history, warning those who would follow love and goodness what kind of fate they can expect. Or the cross can be a beginning on the road to the greatest redemption and hope that history has ever provided. I would not be writing these words and the entire Christian enterprise would be pure fraud if Jesus did not rise from the dead. Jesus' death was not what transformed and sustained his disciples and millions upon millions from that day to this. Jesus' resurrection, his rising from the dead, was the critical event that transmuted utter tragedy to never-ending victory.

Resurrection alone does not bring transformation. It was rather the resurrection of this human being, this special human being, God incarnated in a human soul and body, preaching and living love and mercy, willing to endure all that evil could do to break love's power. Resurrection affirms and clarifies the nature of God, the divine Lover, "love divine all loves excelling, joy from heaven to earth come down." And so we come to the central act in the divine drama. But how on earth can any of us rational, sensible human beings believe in resurrection?

6.

Resurrection

In order to appreciate the depth and power of Jesus' resurrection let us step back into the lives of his desolate friends and followers. Jesus had suffered and died. Let us enter imaginatively into their agony and then watch their transformation as they confront the empty tomb and the appearances of Jesus to them.

Saturday, the sabbath, was nearly as unbearable as Friday, the day of crucifixion. The shock of Friday began to wear off and now they experienced fully their utter despair and grief. The person whom they loved was dead. They had watched him suffer and die. The sword pierced through his mother's heart and the hearts of his friends and disciples. His excruciating death destroyed the one they loved as well as their very reason for living. Their religious foundations crumbled and were washed away in a river of tears. He had spoken of a God of love, a divine Lover, but if such a God existed this God did not intervene in this world. Doubts clawed their way into their minds. Could Jesus have been wrong? Was he deceived? Were they wrong to have given up their ordinary lives to follow him?

Agony swept over them on the sabbath when they could do no work. They were like criminals in solitary confinement with nothing to think about but the horror of their misbegotten lives. The disciples huddled together in a rented house. Each knock at the door brought terror. They imagined that they heard the sound of marching feet, soldiers, the temple guard; they imagined more crosses stark against the sky. The women were more fortunate. They had something to do. They made plans for his embalming, for how they would secure the spices, the myrrh and

81

labdanum. (Funeral preparations can have real psychological value!) Friday night none of them slept; the pain was intolerable, but the sabbath night their bodies were kinder and they slept in spite of their torment.

Judas went out and hanged himself. Poor Judas, he was such a complicated mixture of conflicting motives and emotions. His action was a natural reaction to the hopeless darkness that devoured him. The best attempt to portray the development of this tragic character is found in Dorothy Sayers' remarkable series of radio plays, *The Man Born To Be King*. These dramas were produced by the B.B.C. during the blitz of London. Who was this man Judas whom Jesus selected for his gifts and potential and who like Satan (one of God's finest creations) went wrong and brought tragedy and mayhem into the world? The powers of evil had their day; they possessed and defeated Judas even though they were defeated in the process.[1]

Judas may have been a disciple of John the Baptist invited to join Jesus' band of followers at the time of John's imprisonment. He was able, brilliant, enthusiastic. He handled the treasury for the little fellowship. Whether he sought out the religious leaders who wished to get rid of Jesus or whether they sought him out we don't know. But somehow Judas and Caiaphas came together and Judas was given thirty pieces of silver to betray his master (the price for the freeing of a slave). He left their last supper together and went out to the temple precincts, and from there he led the band empowered to seize Jesus and bring him in for trial. They planned to seize him at night, for Jesus' many followers among the common people would be safely in bed and so would not be aroused. Judas led the temple guard to Jesus' secret rendezvous in the Garden of Gesthemane, went up to Jesus and kissed him.

What were Judas' motives? Like yours and mine they were mixed. Part of him had come to believe that Jesus might be an impostor, a fraud, that he appeared to be someone he was not. Another part felt that Jesus was not stepping into his messiahship as he should and that Judas' act might force Jesus into action. Still another fragment of his being (of which he may not even have been conscious) was angry because Peter, and not he, was called the Rock. Still another contributing factor was his inability to say no when he met with Caiaphas. His hand itched for the money.

He loved and hated at the same time. He probably never thought that his action would lead to crucifixion. Unfortunately our human emotions are not logical and can be totally ambivalent. How often we betray those closest to us through no clearly conscious motive, carried along like Judas by the forces of the unconscious of which we are not aware. Jung has suggested that the essence of sin may lie in unconsciousness that opens us to evil as well as good, and sweeps us along without our knowing where we are moving or why.

Judas had watched from afar and saw them take down the dead bodies from their crosses. All night he tossed and turned, more and more aware of the evil that he had done. He could find no defense for himself, and since Jesus' message of God's unfathomable love had not touched his deepest nature, his despair grew deeper and deeper. In the morning he tried to return the money to the temple officials and they laughed at him. He could imagine no resolution to his situation. How could he ever face those intimate friends of three days before? They might even kill him. The black mood, the hopelessness, became intolerable. Judas betrayed himself. He went out and hanged himself. When the disciples gathered together to select a successor to Judas, Peter told an even more bitter account of Judas' death than we find in Matthew's Gospel. The tragic irony of Judas' death was that had he carried his despair one day longer, Jesus might well have come to him and transformed him as he came with new life on Easter to those who abandoned and denied him.

The Empty Tomb

On the first day of the week, just as the sun was rising and the dawn gave them enough light to find their way, Mary of Magdala, Mary the mother of Jesus and Salome gathered up the embalming spices they had purchased the night before when the sabbath ended at sunset. They set out for the tomb to embalm the body. As they walked along they were talking with one another, heartbroken, discussing how they would remove the great stone that closed the tomb. As the tomb came into sight they were struck with fear and amazement. *The stone was rolled away.*

They ran the last hundred yards. Two of the women entered the tomb. The body was gone. In the place where Jesus' body had been laid they saw a young man of frightening majesty and beauty, an angelic being, a messenger of God. He was sitting on the right side wearing a white robe. Whenever humans meet the divine they are frightened. The women were dumbfounded and the angel hastened to reassure them and tried to reach out to them in their terror. "Do not be afraid. You are looking for Jesus of Nazareth who was crucified. Look, here is the place where they laid him. He is risen. He is not here. Go now and give this message to his disciples and Peter: 'He will go on before you into Galilee, and you will see him there, just as he told you.' "

These words frightened the women even more than the dazzling presence of the holy being. It was too much. They could not comprehend what they had encountered. They dashed out of the tomb beside themselves with amazement and terror. They ran away and at first said nothing to anybody, for they were terrified. Most ancient texts of Mark's Gospel conclude with these surprising words. Whether there was another final page that is missing or whether the experiences of the resurrection were considered too holy to be written, we do not know. I believe that Luke tells the story much as it happened. He also tells of the consternation of the women at their meeting with the angel or angels. They did not go immediately to the disciples, fearing that they would be considered silly women; and when they did tell their story, it appeared to the disciples as nonsense. They just could not believe it.

I had read the story dozens and dozens of times before I perceived what was actually written. The women at the empty tomb panicked and ran away. Only when we are touched by a similar fear can we appreciate the depth and power of the resurrection. Had most of us been making up this story we would have written it quite differently. We would have probably concluded it something like this: "And when the women saw the shining divine messenger sitting in the tomb they were astonished, but the holy being spoke to them and told them that Jesus had risen from the dead and they were to go and tell the disciples and go to Galilee to meet him. At these words the women wept for joy and threw their arms around each other. For a few moments they were si-

lent in their joy, and then cries of joy and exultation broke forth
from their lips: 'He is risen, He is risen. The Lord is risen indeed.' Then they dashed forth from the tomb with light steps and
ran down the hillside calling out to everyone they met: 'He is
risen. He is risen indeed, alleluia.' They found the disciples and
they rejoiced at the good news the women brought; soon after-
ward they all set off for Galilee."

But this is not the way the Gospel tells it. The women were
terrified and ran off, telling no one because they were afraid. And
they had reason to be afraid. Remember what they had been
through—the seizure of Jesus in the garden, a trial before the
Sanhedrin, sentencing before Pilate, the hours of watching him
die on the cross, the derision of the crowd, sleepless nights and
dark hopeless days. Then they met the dazzling holiness in the
tomb. They had given up any hope as they took the broken body
from the cross. They had not been present when Jesus predicted
his passion and rising from the dead, and you can be sure that the
disciples did not understand Jesus enough to share such dark
forebodings. They needed Jesus' humanness to soften the fearful
intensity of the holy. They would get this later, but now they
were simply overwhelmed. They were torn between doubt and
fear. If it were true, and that bright immensity that encountered
them could not be denied, then they had built their lives on all
the wrong assumptions. Suddenly they were confronted with a
world in which God was more powerful than the temple or Rome
or any power. And what is more, God cared what was going on
among human beings and *did something about it*.

Of course a part of them rejoiced in the hope that Jesus had
risen, but still more of them were stupefied, paralyzed with fear.
The world was the way Jesus had described it. They had never
quite believed him. It is all well and good to talk about spiritual
things and spiritual powers, to carry on long and involved discussions about spiritual reality. It is another matter to find ourselves in the hand of the living God who has made heaven and
earth, who has stretched out the stars and fashioned the uncanny
intricacy of subatomic particles. To find that this one cares about
us and is watching with us sends chills down our spines and
shocks of amazement through our hearts.

The first reaction of the women was dread. The initial reaction of any who truly get the message of Easter and the resurrection is likely to be fear. The resurrection was not a sentimental Easter card, but a profound revolution and revelation, an awe-filled one. The incredible love of God in the risen Jesus assumes its deepest significance as it springs out of our fear and amazement. Those of us who have met this risen Jesus in deep despair and are raised out of it have already been terrified and yet such love still amazes us.

Many people turn away from the resurrection because of its frightening aspect. They would prefer to have life knowable and tame and ordered, at least partially within their control. If the resurrection is true, then this world is not what it seems and I may be called upon to follow the way of love revealed in this event. Love may demand all of me, and this will require courage, the kind of courage that the first disciples of Jesus exhibited as they went out with their good news into a hostile and persecuting empire.

Peter and John

Mary Magdalene did not enter the tomb with the other women. Her only thought was that someone had stolen the body away, and in utter despair she dropped her bundles of spices and ran off to find Peter. She found Peter and John together and blurted out that the tomb was open and someone had evidently taken the body from the tomb; she had no idea where they had placed it. Peter and John set right off toward the tomb. They were running side by side, but John was younger and faster and reached the tomb before Peter. He looked in and saw the strange orderliness of the grave wrappings lying quite undisturbed. He was also struck by the electrifying numinous quality within the tomb and hesitated to enter.

Impulsive Peter came up moments later and rushed head-long into the tomb. He, too, noted the order which reigned there. Whatever else, this was not the work of grave robbers. He examined the linen shroud carefully folded and the cloth that had been about Jesus' head rolled up as it had been around his head. John then entered the tomb. Something within him responded to what he saw there and to something more than his eyes were seeing. Jesus' intimations about dying and rising on the third day came back to him. He saw and believed. Perhaps he sensed the presence of the risen Jesus. Peter felt hope rise within his heart and yet he was afraid that hope was vain. He and John looked at each other. The look said to each of them: "We must go and tell the others what we have discovered." Both of them were wrapped deep in thought as they emerged from the tomb and started back to find the others. John was expectant; Peter was torn between doubt and hope.

One thing was sure. Finding the tomb empty was not enough. It was necessary, because without it Jesus' appearances would simply be like other appearances of deceased people at the time of their deaths or later. These are comforting and helpful and in a sense show that death is not final, but they tell us nothing about conquering death in this world in the here and now. The resurrection of Jesus was far more than just an appearance of a deceased person after death while the body lies in the funeral home. The resurrection of Jesus was both *spiritual and physical*. The physical body was transformed into something far more glorious. The worlds of the physical and spiritual met and joined. Creation was totally complete.

Had there been only the empty tomb with its neatly laid out grave clothes and angels, only the spiritually attuned, people like John, would believe. God knew that we human beings need more than authority and inferences if we are going to believe that Love is real, powerful, death-conquering. God knew that we human beings need to have experiences as well as being told and need logically to think it all out. Without the convincing (to be convinced means to be conquered by) and overpowering experiences of the risen Jesus, the victorious Christ, there would have been no courageous Christian Church to pit itself against the Roman Empire. In only three centuries the Christians conquered that Empire in spite of persecution, torture and ridicule. Without the resurrection they would not have believed that their master was indeed the incarnation of God and worth dying for. This is a matter of *both/and* and not *either/or*. Both empty tomb and meetings with the risen Jesus were necessary for a victorious Christianity. The early Church knew this well when it fought against the gnostic belief that God *only appeared* to be incarnate and to die on the cross. The coming of God in the flesh and the resurrection told the disciples (and tells us) that this physical world is God's world and that Divine Love has ultimate power in both. It speaks to the ultimate unity of the world in which we live.

Mary of Magdala

Mary of Magdala was in no condition to make inferences about a risen Jesus. She needed him. Let us go on to the experience that touched and transformed Mary. After finding Peter and John she walked back slowly toward the sepulchre. From a distance she saw them enter and then come out, deep in thought. They did not notice Mary and walked away toward Jerusalem by another way. Mary was crying all the way back to the grave, and she stood beside the entrance weeping as if her eyes were a bottomless well of tears.

Mary had been lost. Most people looking at her would have shaken their heads and said that there was no point trying to help her. Luke—who may have known her well—wrote that she was the one from whom Jesus cast out seven devils. Whatever else to be possessed and delivered from seven devils means, it means that she had been sick in body, soul and mind. She had fallen into utter depravity. She was morally lost, and the lostness of her soul led her into such anguish of mind that she became mentally sick. The sickness of her mind wracked her body and she was tormented and ill. Mary was broken, poor in spirit, worthless. And Jesus healed her.

Tradition identifies her with the brazen woman who broke into the dinner party given by Simon the Pharisee, something no decent woman would have done. She went behind Jesus as he reclined to eat, broke open an alabaster vase, and poured the precious ointment out on him; she washed his feet with her tears and wiped them with her hair. Mary had fallen in every way and considered herself as hopeless as others considered her. She was indeed tormented by seven spirits of weakness and sin, but Jesus cast them out and Mary was whole again. No wonder she burst in upon that party. She had to let him know. The host watched, shocked that this man would let such a woman touch him. Jesus read his thoughts and told a story about forgiveness and then spoke a new truth: Those who are forgiven the most are the most blessed—the mystery of human brokenness and failure.

The tears continued to flow as she came back to the tomb again. She was thinking to herself: "He saved me and I thought I had found meaning, hope and life. I believed that he was God incarnate. He was like God to me. And I was a fool again. It was all illusion, all a sham. I was deceived again, but this time by a noble person. I saw in him more than was actually there, and he was just a noble man. The world and its hurting people can't stand nobility. They destroy it. They destroyed him and they have destroyed me too. Still I will go back to the tomb and see if I can find his body and do what I can."

Mary was confused and desperate. When we can identify with what she was going through, then we can understand Mary's actions. What a comfort it is for me in my darkness and most helpless moments, when everything has caved in on me and I see no hope, to accompany Mary to that empty tomb in my heart and imagination. I can stoop down with her and look into the tomb. There she did not find his body. She did not even see the grave clothes. Two majestic shining white figures were seated—one where his head had been, another at the foot of the slab. Ordinarily such numinous figures would have sent chills of terror through her. But Mary was too full of grief to be shaken by the strange quality of these figures. She could not have been more frightened or despairing; indeed if they had destroyed her at that moment, it would have only been relief. One of them broke the silence with these words: "Woman, why are you weeping?"

At this a fresh flood of tears poured from Mary's eyes. She caught her breath and explained: "They have taken my Lord's body and I do not know where they put him." It is bad enough to lose the one you loved. It is worse to see life crash in because everything that the dead one stood for appeared to have been unreal. But now they had stolen away his body; the only thing left to touch had been snatched away. Mary needed to anoint the broken body of her friend and master; this service for the dead might ease the pain and bring closure to her grief. Taking away the body was the final desecration. Not being able to perform the last ritual was the end of the road, the last indignity, a final stab at her heart. No wonder she wept. Her eyes were so blurred that she was not sure what she had seen within the tomb. Mary had held herself together during the actual nailing to the cross and the hours that he hung there. She had helped take down his body and carry it to the tomb. But now that she found his body gone, she was hysterical with pain and anguish.

She did not know what to make of those creatures in the tomb. What a silly question they asked about her weeping. She stood up and turned around and nearly bumped into a man standing behind her. He was wearing peasant clothes and she thought he must be the gardener who had come early after the sabbath to tend the garden. He also spoke to her: "Woman, why are you crying? Who is it that you are looking for?" They seemed like matter-of-fact questions at the time. Only later did the memory of them reveal to her the touch of divine irony. For several minutes her only answer was another deluge of tears. At length she controlled herself enough to speak. In a pleading voice she asked him: "If you took him away, sir, tell me where you have put him and I will go and get him." She was looking right at Jesus but she was separated from him by a veil of tears and unbelief. She turned away in hopelessness when he did not answer her.

And then he spoke one simple word: "Mary." He called her by her own name. Then she recognized that voice. He had spoken that name with warmth and care when others spoke it only with scorn and derision. It was that voice that had first broken through the wall around her heart. She had determined that no one would ever enter that heart again, but this voice had knocked so quietly that she had let him in. Then came the agony of coming back to life again, like stepping on a leg that had gone to sleep. Now he spoke her name again, and this time the voice brought only joy and peace. The tears dried up, and a smile of unearthly joy lit up her entire face—from darkest night to sunny noonday in one moment.

I need to listen again and again to the way that she cried out: "Rabboni!" Each syllable had a new quality. It was like a bird song. She had always called him Rabboni or Teacher. She wiped the rest of the tears from her face with one quick gesture and stretched out her arms to embrace him. The body that she had come to anoint for burial was standing there before her, radiant in health, glowing like the rays of the rising sun just now beginning to bathe the garden in light.

Then Jesus spoke softly to her: "Not yet, Mary. Do not hold on to me, because I have not yet gone back up to my Father. But go to my brothers and sisters and tell them for me what you have experienced, and tell them that I go back to my Father and your Father, to my God and your God." Mary needed to cease clinging to Jesus' human body and she got the message. Then he vanished from her sight. It all made sense to her now. Mary threw back her head and sang. She danced down the hill; she was chanting: "Rabboni, Rabboni!" She knew that he was the teacher, the master, the lord, the conqueror, God. She had been right to let that voice break into the sealed fortress of her heart. Meaning and love and hope were real. People did not just use one another. The universe did not just use people and cast them off. What a beautiful morning it was. The flowers were blooming in the garden, primroses and wild lilies, roses, red and white; she was as alive as they were. How green the world was.

She found the disciples huddled together with some friends, and she told them: "I have seen the Lord." They smiled indulgent smiles, thinking to themselves that pain works in strange ways on some people's minds. They were courteous. They did not tell her that she was dreaming or crazy. But it didn't bother Mary because she knew, really knew. She knew that he was alive; there was nothing left to fear, not even death or grief or pain or anything. Jesus came to them later and it was Mary's turn to smile. The same kind of transforming experience continued on through the apostolic age and then down through the centuries and still happens today. The gift of the Holy Spirit means many things. One most important aspect of its reality is bringing us experiences of this rescuing and saving risen Christ.

Mary's experience of the risen Jesus gives an enlarged picture of the deepest and most powerful kind of religious experience. In another place I have described nine elements of genuine religious experience.

1. These experiences cannot be adequately described.
2. They give knowledge that is new to the experiencer; they are noetic.
3. They are passive; they are simply given and not self-created.
4. These experiences come and go and we cannot remain within them; they are transient.
5. There is an overwhelming attractiveness to them which draws us to them.
6. At the same time there is a holy fear; we are overwhelmed by holy awe. In *The Idea of the Holy* Rudolf Otto describes the experience of the divine or the holy as the *mysterium tremendum*.
7. The divine may be experienced either as a dazzling darkness or in quite clear and distinct images.
8. Often this experience is described as an experience of ravishing love, of meeting a divine Lover whose justice is consummated in self-giving love.
9. In the deepest experience of many people this love is saving love that lifts us out of inner darkness and torment and even delivers us from out of disaster; it is transforming and saving.

After working on the resurrection for nearly a year I would add a tenth aspect of the most profound religious experience. Our experience demands a response and is not complete until we do respond.[2]

Reflecting on the Resurrection

Before we go on to the rest of the Easter story let us reflect on these three accounts of the resurrection. Such pondering can make it easier for us to assimilate all aspects of this bewildering merging of time and eternity, of physicality and spirituality.

What are we to make of these three stories? One theoretical physicist has said that those who are not shocked and upset by quantum mechanics do not understand it. Unless the resurrection shakes us, confuses and upsets us, we have not truly confronted it. Quantum mechanics tells us that our world is not at all what we ordinarily experience it to be. Light is both a particle and a wave. Matter consists of quanta of energy. Such ideas boggle our minds. They don't fit in our ordered and rational way of looking at things. The resurrection does not fit into our ordinary perceptions of human power and importance and value. The resurrection tells us that at the heart and center of the universe love is reigning. Something deep within us resonates with this radical view of the nature of things in spite of all the evidence to the contrary. James Russell Lowell has expressed this faith in his great hymn:

> Though the cause of evil prosper,
>   Yet 'tis truth alone is strong;
> Though his portion be the scaffold,
>   And upon the throne be wrong,
> Yet that scaffold sways the future,
>   And, behind the dim unknown,
> Standeth God within the shadow
>   Keeping watch above their own.

Why is the resurrection so difficult for us to imagine or believe? There are many reasons, and before we go on to the other accounts of the resurrection, let us look at the objections that many people raise to this incredible event. Many object that resurrection is simply impossible in terms of physical law and what we know about the world around us. A second criticism points to the conflicting nature of the various stories surrounding the resurrection and to their mythical character. The resurrection of the body is bad enough, but there are angels, disappearing acts, passing through doors and then a bodily ascension. Some critics complain that the Gospel of Mark (the earliest Gospel) ends with the women fleeing frightened from the tomb. They suggest that the disciples simply stole the body away and nothing else occurred. Christianity is essentially based upon a fraud. They cannot imagine a resurrected body. And then there are the biblical critics who argue that the empty tomb story is a later development and only the "spiritual" appearances of Jesus to his friends and disciples were real. How can the resurrection have been both physical and spiritual? And last of all there are those who suggest that if anything like a resurrection had really happened, it would have attracted so much attention that it could not have been hidden. Let us look at each of these objections one by one.

There was a time when physicists thought that they really understood our natural world and what could and could not happen within it. This time has passed. There are so many loose ends, so many unanswered questions, so many accepted hypotheses that do not fit together. Some physicists even turn to the East and suggest that the material world may be only a construct of our minds. In addition there is the wide range of data about our capacities to experience in other ways than through sense experience. Human beings do have other ways of experiencing past and present and non-material beings. Reports of near-death experiences and of contact with the deceased are universal. Human beings have experiences of transcendence, of reality beyond the human. These experiences have been transforming and have always given men and women new hope and vision. In *The Two Sources of Morality and Religion* Bergson reminds us that "there is no conceivable means of establishing the impossibility of a fact."[3] If it is possible for human beings to deny extrasensory perception and ordinary experiences of the deceased, how much more difficult for them to believe in a once-only happening like the incarnation and resurrection. And yet is this completion of creation any less likely than other once-only realities like the unbelievably complex organization of matter in the universe or the emergence of life and human knowing?

We have a tendency to believe what is most comfortable for us to believe, as T.S. Kuhn has shown with great clarity in his book *The Structure of Scientific Revolutions*. What we do not expect to see we simply do not perceive; what we don't want to see has two strikes against our perceiving it. The leading edge of the modern scientific community is much more open to possibilities even though there is a rear-guard action on the part of hidebound materialists and determinists that seeks to block us from understanding the mysterious nature of the universe that is opening up to us. Vital, transforming Christian faith is inevitably linked to the resurrection of Jesus. Those who wish to present the resurrection to modern people need to know the comforting humility of some of the greatest scientific minds. I have described this thinking in several books.[4] There was a time when science was a dogmatic adversary of religion and of Christianity in particular. However, with thinkers like Werner Heisenberg, T.S. Kuhn and Robert Oppenheimer we find ourselves in an open universe, with some of the scientists themselves opting for a human soul and a God who can bring us to our full potential.[5] Truly agnostic science can be a handmaid of Christianity and even of the resurrection faith, for it is agnostic about the conclusions of science itself.

We have already mentioned the variety of different accounts found in Paul and in the four Gospel narratives. I repeat what I said before: If each of the writers provided the same identical or similar experiences I would be very dubious of the whole story. Human witnessing particularly under the stress of emotion is a faulty process. This is one reason for the development of a scientific method. But we cannot develop a scientific method to deal with things that are not objectively verifiable, or things that happen only once. We need to rejoice in this marvelous, rich and very human variety of the resurrection stories. Then we need to read them carefully and often to discover those which touch us the most deeply, which appeal to our sense of history and reality. Perhaps this variety was provided by divine wisdom because the Divine Lover knew how different we human beings are and how we need to be reached in very different ways.

As I have meditated on the resurrection for several months, I have been truly amazed at how little the stories conflict with each other. The more I immerse myself in them the more a convincing, progressive account has emerged before me. I had never before tried to do this, and this writing has had a powerful impact upon me.

The mythical quality of the resurrection events is another matter. What about the angels, or Jesus warning Mary not to touch him? What about Jesus going through doors and suddenly disappearing or appearing? Most of us have been so well raised in our materialistic environment that it is difficult for us to imagine anything being real that is not physical. The idea that both physical and spiritual are real boggles our minds. The idea that these realities can be different aspects of each other is still harder for us to understand. We have dreamed and daydreamed about being able to move out of bondage to the hard, cold reality of a pinching and difficult physical world. We wonder if these stories are not just another fantasy. However, our daydreams and fantasies seldom make much change in the world. The people around Jesus, on the other hand, were transformed by their experience of the angels and his mysterious spiritual-physical body.

The Bible is full of angels; they were the messengers of God, beings of essentially spiritual nature who have power in both the spiritual and physical worlds and who could be experienced by human beings. The how-many-angels-can-dance-on-the-head-of-a-pin controversy misses the whole point. It is an attempt to somehow make them physical beings, but they are from a different realm, a different mode of being. It is like asking how many egos can dance on a pin. The ego is not physical, yet my essential "I-ness" can move out into the physical world and even blow it up with nuclear warheads, or it can reach out into the spiritual realm in meditation and prayer. If there was ever an appropriate place for an angel it would have been at the resurrection to announce the good news of what had happened. Do people still experience them? Do they have an effect upon our lives? Do such things still happen? According to Karlis Osis and Erlendur Haraldsson the answer is yes. In their book *At the Hour of Death* they outline and analyze the results of their cross-cultural study of afterlife experiences. One of the experiences they recorded again and again is the presence of a more than human, caring, guiding numinous being in the experiences of dying people and those around them. This was true in the United States, in Europe and in India.

Concrete examples put flesh on the bones of such statistics. One of the most impressive experiences of the angelic was told me by a woman at a conference where I was speaking about the numinous experiences people have of the deceased. Almost always when I open up the subject, someone who has been browbeaten by our materialistic culture comes up and with great relief shares an experience of this other dimension of reality. In a letter this woman described how her mother-in-law had appeared to her with two angelic beings at the time of the elder woman's death, but before the writer knew of her death.

> It was a pretty pre-dawn morning filled with the fragrances of spring when I was suddenly to find myself wide awake and sitting bolt upright in my bed. The room had taken on a rare

atmosphere glistening with a white light tinged with gold. An air of expectancy permeated the room, so much that it made me turn my gaze questioningly to the window at my left, then to those directly across from me, and at that moment, just to the right, this scene appeared.

Two beings of stately yet gentle bearing, almost as tall as the room is high in that area, stood facing each other on either side of a large doorway. They were clothed, each one, in a soft, flowing opaque garment with a radiance resembling sunshine on snow tinged with a faint pink. Their arms seemed wing-like, reaching from their shoulders almost to the floor.

They stood silent and motionless, and yet in a state of expectancy (I seemed to sense) until a feminine figure garbed in a darker hue came into view, with head bent slightly down and forward as if slowly ascending from a lower level. They then moved to enfold her, almost caressingly—and I distinctly saw the smiling face of our mother and heard her familiar voice laughingly say, as if a bit breathlessly, "I've finally made it!" She seemed happy. The smile remained on her face, as, still enfolded in their embrace, she and the two beings *glided* by me . . . just inches from the foot of my bed. I reached out to touch her. My heart cried, "Mother, Mother, don't you see me?" Taking no notice of me they glided on by and out of sight.

The room was scintillating. In fact my whole being seemed charged with a force that I had never known before . . . I felt electrified—even the room seemed electrified. I don't know any other word to describe it.

The atmosphere in the room was changing now, becoming more normal, although it still remained charged and my body still seemed all aglow. As a matter of fact, this lasted to a degree for several days.

At this moment the phone rang to tell of her mother-in-law's unexpected death. She concluded her letter by saying that she wished she might paint a picture of those angelic beings. "Even now," she wrote, "the mere thought of them stirs my soul."[6]

Sometimes a dream can bring us an encounter with this other dimension of reality with the same power as this vision. Several years ago I received a letter from a mother whose teenage son had been killed in tragic circumstances. In a dream-vision two pictures or scenes appeared in which her son Michael was present with intense reality. He appeared and disappeared in much the same way that Jesus appeared and disappeared in the Gospels. "Then he reappeared sitting on the side of the pool table about a foot from me doing one of his trick shots. I put out my arms and he fell toward me and said, 'Oh, Mom, someone cut off my breath.' Before he fell into my arms he disappeared, and I was just standing there." At first her son was very happy, but not as she reached out to him. She remembered thinking that she didn't even get to touch or feel him. After that her husband went to work and she went into the kitchen next to the pool room and noticed that the atmosphere "was so electrifying. It is hard to put into words how it felt. I felt a little uncomfortable or frightened."[7]

Where people have not been brainwashed by the materialism of our Western culture, people often tell of such experiences; these experiences are really quite common. Undoubtedly human beings sometimes exaggerate these experiences as they do descriptions of heroic happenings in the space-time world. The words myth or mythological are only derogatory when they mean (as Bultmann maintains) a contact with a spiritual dimension which *in fact we don't have*. Once we get out of that nineteenth century mentality, myth is a description of our contacts, factual contacts, with other dimensions of reality that people had in Jesus' time and still have.

These happenings in our time can shed light upon what happened at the empty tomb. The women who first came there found an empty tomb, and the angels—appearing as scintillating young men—spoke to them telling them not to be afraid (one of the first things that genuine angelic beings usually do, as they know their presence is uncanny, awesome and frightening). Then the angels told them what to do. They were evidently not ready to experience the risen Jesus. It would have been too much for them. Perhaps one reason that Mark says no more about the experiences of the resurrected Jesus was that it was hard to find words to describe so wonderful an event. Or perhaps he was speaking to people already well informed on these encounters. He knew that his descriptions could not compare with that. For this latter group Mark sets down in writing what he remembered and what Peter had told him about the death and life of Jesus so that these details would not be forgotten, but these were clearly secondary to the saving encounter with the risen Jesus. Or the last pages of Mark may have been lost. How important it is for us to remind ourselves as we read the New Testament that the resurrected Christ was so real to those early Christians who experienced him, meeting, directing and saving them, that they did not find it necessary to distinguish between what they remembered of the historical Jesus and what they experienced of him resurrected in the here and now.

Evidently John and Peter did not perceive the angels that the women had seen in the *reality* of a vision. But something about the empty tomb touched them. It was most likely pervaded with the same kind of numinous power (only infinitely multiplied) described in the two letters. How deeply touched I was as I knelt in prayer in the tomb in the Church of the Holy Sepulchre in Jerusalem. There was something truly holy there, whether it was the actual tomb or not. John knew that something marvelous had happened in that tomb and Peter was trying to make sense of his experience.

Mary saw two angels, but even their holiness was wasted on her and she was no better for the experience. She was looking only for a dead body and so she did not even recognize Jesus when *he came seeking her*. When she came to her senses her only thought was similar to that of Michael's mother in the dream, to touch and hold him as she had when she anointed him and washed his feet with her tears and wiped them with her hair. The mother needed to let go of her son and go on in life. Mary needed to realize that she had encountered something more than an ordinary physical body. It might have been too much for her to have seized that much holiness. Then Jesus disappeared and Mary went to find the disciples.

Let us now look at the argument that the only evidence in Mark is an empty tomb and that this could be explained by fraud or grave-robbers. One of the main reasons why people opt for this solution to the problem is that they simply cannot imagine how a physical body could disappear or turn into a resurrected one—the old bugaboo of materialism unenlightened by modern physics. I don't have a motion picture of what happened, and I wonder if this event might have not blasted the film equipment, but we can present a good imaginative guess of what did occur. Our rational, Western minds deserve the best description we can provide.

The very best presentation of the events surrounding the resurrection of Jesus is by the gifted Christian scholar and detective story writer, Dorothy Sayers. She weaves the various accounts together into a meaningful and understandable play, the twelfth and last of her plays, in *The Man Born To Be King*. This play, "The King Comes To His Own," could be used effectively in any Christian congregation at Easter. She recognizes the difficulties in presenting events of this magnitude and provides a note at the beginning of this play which deals honestly and in depth with these difficulties. She writes:

> The problem here has been to present, in one way or another, no fewer than nine supernatural appearances, without tedious repetition, and without suggesting either Surrey melodrama or the more lily-livered kind of Easter card. The treatment has been varied as frequently as possible between narrative and direct presentation; and an attempt has been made to distinguish between two elements which appear mingled in the narratives about the Risen Body—a queerness on the one hand and an odd kind of homeliness on the other. Though It appeared and vanished in a startling manner, and though Its identity was never immediately recognisable, the Body does not seem to have surrounded Itself with any atmosphere of numinous horror, and indeed took pains to establish Its essential humanity, by eating and allowing Itself to be handled. Only at Its appearance by the Sea of Galilee (presumably towards the end of the 40 days, when It was preparing to leave the earth) does the queerness become dominant over the homeliness.
>
> As against this, the Angels seem on at least two occasions to have established a genuine supernatural awe—the women at the tomb "were afraid and bowed down their faces" and the "keepers trembled and were as dead men."
>
> I have tried to set the key for this in the remark made by the Levit Joel: "The thing (the Risen Body) that passed us in the garden was human, but this (the Angel) was not."

Mechanics of the Resurrection: While it is unnecessary, either for faith or morals, to have any fixed views on the physical mechanism of the Resurrection, it is better for the artist to have some sort of consistent picture in his mind. The operative elements in the problem are (1) the open sepulchre (2) the undisturbed graveclothes. Why this conjunction?

(1) It seems clear that the rolling back of the stone by the Angel was not done to let the Body out. A form that could pass through barred doors or vanish into thin air from the supper-table was not going to be baulked by a few hundred-weight of stone. The door was opened in order to draw the attention of the guards and the disciples to the fact that the Body was gone.

(2) But since the removal of the stone destroyed the evidence of the unbroken seals and lent itself to a naturalistic explanation of the miracle, the grave-bands were left still in their windings for inspection.

Consequently, we can presume that when the Angel rolled back the stone, it was to disclose the tomb *already empty.*

We may therefore suppose that the physical body was, as it were, dissolved into its molecular elements, drawn out through the graveclothes and through the stone, and reassembled outside—this phenomenon being (not surprisingly) accompanied by a violent "electrical" disturbance, perceptible as a kind of earthquake.

This, at any rate, is the picture which I have tried to give. The guards feel the tremors, and, on touching the stone, are sensible of some sort of molecular disturbance; and in the next moment this "electric storm" passes out through the stone, flinging them apart with shock. At nine feet the Body is materialised sufficiently to flatten the flame of the torch as It passes over it. At thirty paces, It is already assembled into form and solidity.

There is no reason to imagine that the Body was obliged always to carry Its original physical components about with It. Presumably It could build Itself up from any atomic material that happened to be handy. But the disappearance of the original earthly body was obviously necessary *as evidence.*

It is also clear that the materialisations were always rapid. There are never any slow twirlings and thickenings of gaseous matter, as in the ectoplasmic manifestations of the spiritualist seance. Nor do subsequent appearances seem to have produced any of the "electrical" phenomena that attended the first.

It seemed desirable to establish a terrestrial and commonplace background to this supernatural story by inserting a couple of ordinary human scenes—the Sanhedrin scene and the little scene before the Governor's house—showing the reactions of Jews and Romans to the Resurrection.

Otherwise, the only point to note is that this play contains a good deal about doors, and knockings at doors. It is, in fact, a play about the door between two worlds.[8]

I cannot add much to this superb description except to note that it was written before quantum mechanics. The threat of nuclear annihilation reminds us entirely too clearly how energy and mass are interchangeable. This brings us to the problem of the physical and visionary (non-material) aspects of the resurrected Jesus.

We have already indicated that some physicists (like Fritjof Capra in his book *The Tao of Physics*) are so impressed by the *immaterial* quality of matter that they turn to the mystical thinking of Hinduism and Buddhism and suggest that matter may be only the projection and contribution of the human mind. There are certainly similarities between modern physics and mysticism both East and West. How important it is for us to realize that the essential qualities of my typewriter and the table on which it rests as well as of my body and the fingers that are typing are very, very different from what they appear. When we try to picture what matter is really like, we are faced with fully as many problems as understanding the resurrected body of Jesus. Matter is mostly empty space, and then there are those basic quanta of reality (electrons) that can appear as either matter with extension or as waves of energy. The actual "solidity" of a vast stadium could be reduced to the size of a pea if all the empty space were removed. As Heisenberg has demonstrated, the very nature or location of these quanta can never be known as they are in themselves.

We don't have to go so far as to dissolve the physical world into unreality, as the Hindus often do, to begin to see that we live in a very mysterious universe where things like the resurrection are going on all the time on a subatomic level. Certainly the one who made this incredible universe with its quixotic character could have provided his incarnate presence in this world with the strange qualities which are recorded in the resurrection narrative. Again it was probably the need of those to whom the Christ came that dictated how he came. When the disciples needed to be reassured of his physicality and humanness, he appeared in this manner. When the more visionary experience was enough, Jesus appeared in this manner. Some of them needed to know that this resurrection was far more than just an ordinary vision of the deceased. It was a real breakthrough of the divine into the space-time world and it could be experienced in different ways. Those who had been through the terror and horror of Good Friday needed more than ordinary reassurance.

Why did this resurrection make no more impression on the age in which he lived? There are many reasons. First of all, this was an age in which the miraculous was often reported. In such a world the miraculous is just as easily discounted. Those who did not take the trouble to investigate would just nod their heads and consider it another old wives' tale. We have already dealt with the second reason briefly. The phenomenon of cognitive dissonance is widely known. It simply means that we do not perceive certain facts because we have no categories in our thinking processes in which to place them. I have described in other books examples of this human trait of not seeing what is there. The most interesting and startling example involves the use of an ordinary deck of playing cards. Instead of the regular black six of spades a red six of spades was inserted in the deck, and the pack of cards was shown one by one to unsuspecting subjects. Practically no one saw the red six of spades as a red six of spades. The card was usually reported as an ordinary black six of spades or as the six of diamonds or hearts. *What we do not expect to see, we often do not see at all. What does not fit into our understanding of reality we actually are likely not to see.* A trial attorney friend told me that this explained to him why some clients actually did not see the motorcycle they hit; they were looking for cars. If people don't believe what they have seen when it conflicts with *what they think they should observe,* how much less likely are people to believe reports of *happenings* which do not fit, like the resurrection!

Jesus warned his disciples that rising from the dead would not necessarily convince people. The rich man in torment in Hades pleaded with father Abraham to send someone from the dead to warn his brothers who were as unconcerned about the poor as he had been. Abraham answered, "If they do not listen to Moses and the prophets, they will pay no heed even if someone rises from the dead." We human beings don't like to change our basic assumptions about life or reality. T. S. Kuhn notes that scientists who are forced to face facts contrary to their basic theories become very nervous and exhibit many of the symptoms of anxiety. The resurrection of Jesus overturned nearly all of the prevailing assumptions about life and reality current in his time (and, I might add, in our own). This event was an affirmation of the person who taught and lived love; it was a statement that at the heart and center of reality, in the inmost core of God, was love.

The actual reaction of people to resurrection may well be more like that depicted by Eugene O'Neill in his drama, *Lazarus Laughed*. People wanted nothing to do with Lazarus. He interrupted their consuming devotion to trivial things. Mary and Martha were shocked and angry when he laughed at the news of Jesus' death. Finally the world murdered him in order not to be reminded, annoyed, upset. Commenting on both the resurrection of Lazarus and the resurrection of Jesus, Paul Scherer in his exposition of Luke in *The Interpreter's Bible* writes these words: "The Resurrection is a vista that makes our world too small. And it makes human life too great. . . . Whenever a man comes to a huge city from the town back home, where his name was bandied about the streets, and everybody knew his uprising and his downsitting, he is inclined, almost irresistibly inclined, to scuttle in out of the limelight with a sigh of ponderous relief! Nobody knows him, thank God! And nobody cares what he does—thank God again! He can hide now from a thousand responsibilities. Perhaps the doctrine of our insignificance is a kind of wishful thinking! The resurrection makes our dimensions too big."[9] We are far more important than we think if this was done for us. There is no hiding place from Love. This is indeed frightening.

The refusal to see eternal meaning for the human soul in spite of all the evidence to the contrary may well be a cop-out, the fear of having to take eternal responsibility for ourselves. Most people who have experienced near encounters with death and *know* that they did not cease to be are quite careful to whom they tell their experiences. People are shaken by their accounts.

With these reflections on the resurrection of Jesus in mind let us listen to the encounters that the other disciples had with their risen Lord. Once we are potentially open to this amazing happening, we will find one or two of these meetings that are particularly meaningful to us. In addition the total account has an impact that one account cannot have. Paul, in a letter to the Corinthians, wrote these words: "First and foremost, I handed on to you the facts which had been imparted to me: that Christ died for our sins, in accordance with the scriptures; that he was buried; that he was raised to life on the third day, according to the scriptures; and that he appeared to Cephas, and afterwards to the Twelve. Then he appeared to over five hundred of our brothers at once, most of whom are still alive, although some have died. Then he appeared to James, and afterwards to all the apostles." Paul then goes on to tell that Jesus even appeared to him, monstrous as he had been in persecuting the Church.

Jesus Comes to Peter

Paul's letter is the earliest written account of the resurrection; it reports an early appearance of Jesus to Peter which is not recorded in the four Gospels. Like the resurrection this appearance was probably so basic to the spoken Gospel message that it was not thought necessary to write about it in detail. Without it how could Peter have preached with authority? To appreciate the significance of Jesus' encounter with Peter, we need to put ourselves in Peter's shoes as he heard the cock crow the second time.

Just as the cock crowed the second time anguish struck Peter like a knife between his ribs; he had just denied Jesus for the third time. He walked a little way apart and wept bitterly. The tears flooded over his weatherbeaten, wrinkled cheeks. No wonder he wept. He had denied his master. It happened just as Jesus had predicted. All his professions of loyalty flooded back into his mind: "Oh, no, master, I will never leave you. Even if I have to die with you I will not leave you." The tears welled up from the very center of his being, from the bottom of his heart. Was there anything to staunch this flood? Could anything heal the breach in his inner being made by his denials? Would he ever be able to hold his head high again? Weeping and broken, Peter wandered off into the night to find those who had not even had the courage to follow Jesus to trial. They, too, had made bold vows of loyalty.

How many times we feel like Peter. How often we deny the risen Jesus in our speech and actions. Often when confronted with all of ourselves we feel like Peter and wonder if there is any hope for us. One of the reasons we spend so little time in silence is that when we stop and listen to our inner depths we are faced with our betrayals and unconsciousness. If we can stay busy enough we can often avoid facing the many ways we have betrayed our own souls, our God, the Holy Spirit, Jesus, what we know is right and holy and good. We see the noblest people around us go down in defeat, mocked and derided, and we stand by denying or saying nothing. But we suddenly remember what we thought we stood for, and then come the tears and the despair. We are so much like Peter.

Peter remembered the supper at which he had spoken so boldly and his failure to stay awake when Jesus had pleaded with him to give human support. Jesus, in agony, wrestled through the decision of whether he would stay and suffer crucifixion or flee and save his life. The soldiers came and Judas gave his master the kiss of death. For a few moments they were brave: as long as they had swords in their hands. At Jesus' command they put away their swords; and then they fled.

Peter followed the band of soldiers at a distance to the house of Caiaphas and waited in the courtyard outside. A servant girl saw him warming himself over a brazier. She said to him: "You were with this man from Nazareth, Jesus." Peter denied it. Peter might have admitted to the soldiers or to the high priest that he was a follower, but why to this servant? So it is with us. We deny Jesus in little things, to insignificant people, where it does not seem to matter. She asked him a second time and again he denied that he knew him. And then a bystander who heard him speak remarked: "You must be one of them, for your accent is that of a Galilean." And this time Peter cried out with an oath: "I do not know this man you speak of." And the cock crowed, and Peter burst into tears. Can you imagine how Peter felt? To say three times that he did not know Jesus.

Peter fled. He found some of the other disciples hiding in a locked room like dumb and broken animals. Peter was so distraught that he could hardly speak. He did not have the courage to follow Jesus before Pilate or wait at the foot of the cross. He wondered if Jesus really would have wanted him there. Peter had failed. The Twelve had failed.

Could anything make a man of Peter again? What could ever restore his self-respect? What could give him some peace again, some hope for himself? No human action could mend the wound of Peter's denial, no amount of human caring or comfort, counseling or psychiatry. Nothing that Peter did or could do would be able to restore him and make him feel like a decent human being once again. As he waited those dark days Peter doubted that he could ever stop loathing himself. And yet Peter became a courageous man, a saint, one of the foundation stones of the Church that conquered the ancient world. How did it all happen?

Jesus rose from the dead and sought Peter out. Jesus came to Peter radiant with life and wholeness. We do not know the details of this encounter. In that meeting with the risen Jesus of Nazareth, Peter was transformed. He was reborn and started all over again. The past was wiped away. Peter was accepted, forgiven and given a fresh start. His encounter with the loving, risen Jesus told Peter that this is a world of second chances. Jesus' rising from death took away the finality of Peter's denial and failure.

When Peter preached the good news he would say: "If Jesus cared enough for me who denied him to come to me, does he not care for you? Will he not come to you in your need?" Neither our denials nor Peter's can destroy the Spirit; neither can separate us from the risen Christ. He is stronger than our weakness. The resurrection told Peter and those of us like him that we need not despair; it lifts the burden of ourselves from ourselves.

Jesus sought out Mary and he sought out Peter. The risen

Jesus, like the purely human Jesus, loved Peter and came to him and expressed that love. It was not just the implications of resurrection that were important to Peter. His master still cared, loved, forgave, and sought him out, not in spite of his weaknesses and failures but even because of them, because Peter needed him so much. Those who are forgiven the most love the most. The risen Jesus seeks us out in the very same way and stands at the door of our souls knocking and asking to be let in. We can let him in as we receive his body and blood in the Eucharist, as we stop in silence to open the door imaginatively to his knocking, or as we call out in despair for his saving power.

Tradition tells us that Peter stands at the gateway of heaven to let us in. What an unexpected and delightful joy to find Peter there with the keys to the Kingdom around his waist. Christianity is the only religion that offers free forgiveness of sins to those who ask for it and has built this idea into its very creeds. Peter at the gate of heaven reminds me that when I come to that place I will not be asked about all my failures and mistakes, but rather: Will I allow the love portrayed in Jesus' resurrection from death on a cross to touch me and transform me? The power of the resurrection was for Peter an incredible experience of forgiveness, and the same transforming presence is available to us today.

The Stranger on the Road

The first day of the week was a glorious spring day. That only made the pain worse for Cleopas and Simon. Their lives had fallen apart. Jesus was dead. They were going home defeated, broken human beings. How different it had been five days before when they went up to Jerusalem for the Passover to be with Jesus. Both of them had been convinced that the time had arrived for Jesus to establish his Kingdom.

They didn't know how it would happen, but some marvel would take place. The Romans would flee in terror, thrown out. The temple would be purified and the Kingdom of God would be ushered in. They had arranged their affairs so that they could drop everything and follow Jesus wherever he might lead, no matter what happened. If this was not the time, they felt that it would come soon. They would stay with him until he was ready to usher in the new age.

Both of these men had often been with Jesus and his friends. He had healed Simon's brother and Cleopas' daughter. They had never known anyone like him. Before they knew him, their lives had been empty, hopeless. They worked from day to day. The extortion of tax collectors and the power of the rich kept them scratching to stay alive. It is hard to live in an occupied country. One's soul is never really one's own. There is the temptation to join the underground, but that looked even more futile. They couldn't forget the crosses that lined the highways after any rebellion. Rome was very powerful.

Jesus had given them a new vision of what life could be. Simon remarked one day to his friend: "He knows my faults and still he loves me. He seems to love me because I need his love so much. The more he forgives my grasping bitterness and sexual follies, the more I love him." Cleopas replied: "He is kind, warm, unafraid, loving, but he has incredible power too. That power I do not understand. Power and love mixed make an awesome combination. I never thought I would see such a combination. He lives in the world and beyond it at the same time. I wonder if he is an ordinary mortal. He'll bring the Kingdom in a supernatural way."

Now they were discussing how wrong they had been. Jesus was dead. He never raised a finger to fight back. They had spent Thursday night in Bethany and came late Friday morning into Jerusalem. The day was black and wild. Just outside the city walls they saw three men hanging there on crosses. They could hardly believe their eyes. On the central cross hung their master, the king of the age to come, Jesus. They were struck dumb, stupefied, numb. They found some friends in the crowd; they pieced together the story of what had happened. They waited until the end, hoping for some miracle, but Jesus died like the rest of us. They went back to Bethany waiting for the sabbath to pass.

Sunday ultimately arrived and they were going home to Emmaus to muster strength to pick up the pieces and go on living in a meaningless world. As they left the city they went to see the disciples. They actually resented the bright, balmy spring day. It was out of keeping with the world. The darkness of Friday would have been far more appropriate. They trudged on talking about the things they had been through, wondering if there was anything else they should have done. They were halfway home when a stranger caught up with them. They were so deep in agonizing reminiscences that they did not notice him until he was walking alongside them, adjusting to their stride.

For a while all three walked along silently, and then the stranger spoke: "What on earth were you talking about so earnestly back there? It must have been something awful. Your voices were laced with pain." Cleopas and Simon stopped, raised their eyes from the road and looked at the stranger. Then Cleopas said: "Are you the only person coming from Jerusalem who does not know what things happened there the past three days?" Shaking his head, the stranger asked them: "What things are you talking about?"

The story poured out of them, each one filling in details the other had forgotten. They were so grateful for his willingness to listen to their grief and bear its burden with them. It really helped them to tell the story to another. How intently he listened as they spoke: "All this happened to Jesus of Nazareth, a prophet powerful in speech and action before God and the Jewish people. Our chief priests and rulers were jealous and handed him over to be sentenced to death and crucified. But we had been hoping that he was the one to liberate Israel. What is more, this is the third day since all this happened, and this morning some women of our fellowship amazed us with a strange story. They went early to the tomb, but his body was gone and they could not find it. They also told a story that they had seen a vision of angels who told them that he was alive. Some of his disciples immediately went to the tomb and found everything there just as the women had said, but they did not see Jesus. Frankly, it is bad enough to grieve over losing everything without being fed such stories. It's better to face the awful truth that love never wins in this world or maybe even in the next. We just have to grind on until we die."

At this point the stranger broke in. He was almost rude: "How stupid and dull, how foolish you two are. How slow you are to catch the true meaning the prophets have been speaking for centuries. Did they not tell you that the Messiah, the anointed one, the future king of Israel, would have to suffer tragically before he entered into his glorious victory?" The two friends could hardly believe their ears. Then this man went on to reveal the meaning of the Scriptures to them. Their hearts simply burned, hearing the way he explained things. They had only heard one other person ever talk like that before, and he was dead. This stranger had the deep understanding of Scripture that Jesus had. He told them that they had misunderstood the prophets; human beings never win through strength, but rather through weakness. The coming king would naturally have to die before he could assume power over all things. He spoke of the suffering servant, of dying to rise again, of losing one's life to gain it. He showed them how this theme ran right through the Bible. Still they did not make the connection.

The remaining three miles to Emmaus simply vanished while they listened to him. The man told them that love conquers just because it dies willingly. The whole law and the prophets became luminous. Their spines tingled and they quivered and trembled in their inner being. They came to a fork in the road. Cleopas and his friend turned off on the road which led to the village. The stranger started to continue down the other road. Simon called to him: "Sir, why don't you stay here with us. My home is simple but the day is almost over. It is getting dark and we're hungry. You must be also. Come and share our supper with us." They were both embarrassed, for they had never asked the traveler his name, but he seemed happy to be invited. He nodded agreement and came with them to their home.

Simon showed his guest where to wash and then set a table for them. He went out to get several loaves of bread and set them on the table with a jug of wine and cups. They all sat down together. The stranger reached over and took the bread, acting as if he were the host. He said a blessing which they had heard before. He broke the bread and gave them each a piece.

Cleopas and Simon were looking at his hands when he broke the loaf; at the same time they both saw the print of nails in each hand. A shudder of mingled joy and fear passed through them. Their eyes traveled from the hands to the face. The man was a stranger no longer. It was Jesus, the very one they had loved so much, the one who had touched the inmost recesses of their hearts and given them hope. He looked straight into their faces. His face portrayed joy and confidence, compassion and friendship, victory and love. They cried out for joy and reached out to him in amazement and bewilderment, but he vanished from their sight.

Like a storm in the desert the streams of their joy were suddenly running full. In slightly different ways both of them thought they had been carried to the heart of love at the center of the universe. They felt like Dante as he reached the tenth and last circle of heaven and there experienced the consummation of life's meaning:

> Yet, as a wheel moves smoothly, free from jars,
> My will and my desire were turned by love,
> The love that moves the sun and the other stars.[10]

Strange, but Jesus' disappearing did not deflate their joy. His very vanishing meant that he was always present, always there. Cleopas and Simon looked at one another. Without words they knew that they had experienced the resurrected Jesus himself. They both spoke together, almost in unison. "We must go back to the others and let them know that the women were right; they don't need to suffer anymore." They wanted to share what they now knew. Jesus had risen. He died for a purpose and had risen to secure the greatest victory ever won. They left their food and ran most of the seven miles back to Jerusalem.

Why did Jesus appear to these otherwise unknown and unimportant followers on their way home, when he had not as yet even appeared to most of the apostles? Why were Cleopas and Simon selected? Luke doesn't give us the particulars, but we can make some good guesses.

In the first place these two human beings had the courage to pick themselves up and go on. They were broken, but not defeated. Tragedy had befallen them, but they girded their loins and started back to ordinary life again. In my experience people who battle on through life in spite of difficulties are more likely to find God (or be found by the Holy One) than those who give up. Tillich describes this truth well in *The Courage To Be;* courage and persistence can bring us through to an experience of ultimate reality.

In addition they did not abandon what they had experienced as real in Jesus. They remained true to their deepest experience. They didn't just dismiss the whole experience with Jesus and say to each other: "We were fools to have believed in that man. We were duped. Let's never discuss him again. Let's never bother about the ultimate things of life. Let's forget it all." Many people get disillusioned when the going gets rough, but these men cared too much. They continued to struggle through to an understanding of what had happened. They cared about life and they were not about to give up their seeking easily.

Jesus sought them out because they still had open hearts and minds. They hadn't closed their minds with defeat. They were willing to risk being hurt again. They were willing to listen to the stranger who met them on the way and to allow hope to rise like a holy fire within them.

And finally, these two men wouldn't let the stranger go when he began to make some sense to them. When it appeared as if he would go on and leave them, they would not let him go. They hung on to him and entreated him to stay with them. Had they not done so, they might well have missed the most glorious experience of their lives. So many of us get a glimmer of light and then let it fade from us, but not Cleopas and Simon. The stranger accepted their hospitality, took bread and broke it and their eyes were opened.

Jesus, the Christ, still appears to human beings who are open to him, although not often with the startling power with which he appeared to these two. Chesterton tells a similar story about St. Francis of Assisi, who was terrified of leprosy. One day while he was traveling, he saw before him in his path a man white with the dread disease. At first Francis drew back in horror, but he got hold of himself and ran and embraced the leper and then passed on. A moment later Francis looked back and there was no one there. Francis never doubted that it was the Christ himself whom he had encountered there.[11] In a later chapter we shall give

several examples of how the Christ continues to come to floun-
dering men and women and to turn their lives around.

Jesus Comes to His Own

All day Sunday the disciples huddled together behind
locked doors. The stories of the women and of John made little or
no impression. John tried to explain to them the conviction and
hope that had come to him. They listened, politely shaking their
heads. With typical male chauvanism they simply dismissed
Mary's account as the derangement of a simple-minded and
overly-emotional woman. Her very joy and peace confirmed
their judgment about her mental illness. The discussions went
back and forth, going nowhere. The Eleven came and went. During the late afternoon James said: "This is all nice talk, but none
of us has seen him."[12] Andrew had been out of the room. When
he came back he was strangely quiet and then he spoke up in a
low voice: "Peter has seen something." Several of them chimed
in: "What's that, Andrew?"

A hush fell on the room as Peter's brother spoke: "I went to
him just now, and found him stretched upon the floor. He said:
'The Lord is alive; I have seen him.' And I said: 'What, here?' He
answered: 'Yes.' 'Well,' I said, 'what did he say to you?' Peter answered, 'Don't ask.' I laid him on his bed, and he fell instantly
into a deep sleep, like a child. He is asleep now. Thomas is sitting
with him." Impatiently Philip spoke: "It was a vision, maybe, or
a dream. Our Lord is dead." John replied: "Yes, Philip, I said
that too, God forgive me. Yet did we not see the widow's son
raised up and Lazarus called up from the grave? And what did
our Lord say to you at that last Passover supper?" The conversation went on and on, but only John and Andrew spoke with
any conviction. They all wished that it were so, but they could
only believe that it might be so. Nathanael voiced the common
doubt: "You say he's alive, John. Well, what's he doing? And
what are we to do? You know an order has gone out that anybody
who repeats this resurrection story will be put in prison,
and . . ."

At that moment a loud knock shook the door. The disciples looked at one another and Andrew spoke in terror: "It's the end. They've come for us." They wondered what to do; one suggested that they bar the door. Cleopas and Simon knocked again and called out: "Don't be afraid; it is just Cleopas and Simon. We have good news." The door was opened and then locked and barred behind them. The whole story spilled out about the stranger and how Jesus had revealed himself in the breaking of the bread. Cleopas finished: "What a moment, but then in a flash he was gone. There was no one there, but the fragments of the broken bread lay upon the table." When several of the doubters objected that it was just a vision, a ghost, Cleopas reminded them that the bread *had been broken*. Increasing uneasiness was rising among them; the stories they heard were uncanny, frightening and multiplying.

At that moment Jesus appeared there in the midst of them. He spoke his usual familiar greeting: "Hello. Good evening." They first looked startled and then they shrank back terrified, almost afraid to look at him. It was as if they had been thrust into the creative dynamo in the center of the universe, into the heart of being. Numinous awe and fear struck them like a giant wave. Even Cleopas and Simon were a bit afraid as the reality of Jesus and of his glory did not fade away.

Then Jesus stretched out his scarred hands to them and said, "My friends, why are you so troubled? What are you afraid of? Why are you so overcome by doubts? Do you think that I am a ghost come to torment you? My children, it is I, your friend and master. It is I myself. Come, touch me, feel me and see that I am real, a real body. A ghost does not have flesh and bones." Still they were afraid and hung back. He spoke to them again: "Do you have anything to eat?" There was something ludicrous about this numinous reality asking for food, but it broke the spell that their fear had cast upon them. They had a piece of broiled fish; they handed it to him. Right there before them he took the fish and ate it with relish. John was the first to come and touch him. Then they all began to crowd around him, touching his hands and feet. He was the same warm, human Jesus. But there was something else about him, something wonderful, yes, something uncanny, but no longer frightening. They asked him questions and he answered them. He embraced each one of them tenderly. Then he explained the Scriptures to them and the meaning of everything that had happened. He told them that they were to share their new vision of reality. They were to start in Jerusalem and then to go out into the Roman world and even beyond that. He also told them that he would give them the power to do all this. Several hours went by in a split second. He blessed them and then he disappeared in just the same strange way in which he had come. A barred door made no more difference to him than the stone that had sealed the tomb.

Wild joy broke out among them. They hugged one another and cried out again and again: "He is risen. Our Lord is risen indeed." Their brokenness was healed; their guilt was forgiven. They were like men and women released from prison; they were freed from the oppression of despair. In 1839 in Jamaica on the morning of emancipation the former slaves went up to a high hill overlooking the bay to watch the sun rise, the sun which brought them the new day and liberation. At the first rays of the sun their voices broke into a chant: "Free, free, free . . ." The disciples knew this freedom.

Andrew went in to wake Peter and to tell Thomas what had happened. Peter joined in their elation, but Thomas just shook his head in disbelief. Then they unlocked the door and went out in the streets. There was nothing to fear. They sought out the followers of Jesus who were still in the city and they spoke out with courage. Thomas remained behind, saying: "Unless I see the holes made in his hands by the nails and put my finger in them, and until I place my hand in his side, I will not believe."

Thomas Speaks

How often at the right moment the right thing falls into our hands when we are open to receive it. When I was wondering how to tell the story of the skeptical disciple, Thomas, John Brugaletta sent me a poem he had written on the very subject. It said what I wanted to say better than I could. He gave me permission to share Thomas' account of what occurred.

THE BEAST IN BETHANY
(*THOMAS SPEAKS*)

I tell you straight, I am not weak in the hams
As grown men go. I have seen strong men die,
And the weeping and prostrate too, lambs
Of children baffled by the pain while women cry.

You want a fact? Death is a fact.
When death arrives, everything else goes,
As if an absolute and cruel king had lacked
A seat and every good man gave up his. Those

Fragrances of springtime, friendships at a feast,
One's treasure of a wife, some wealth secure,
Fresh bread, the morning birds, the psalms; all yeast
That leavens little pockets in the dusty world, as sure

And stable in the face of death as wind
Or fall's expected crops. A house of twigs. Then came
Our rabbi, one good man who could rescind . . .
But no, I leap ahead. With these two eyes I saw him heal
   the lame.

(By what new power?) Madmen he dispossed of imps,
The blind he sighted . . . on and on. It was like Joy
To be with him, to see the miseries fall flat, to see the
   crimps
He put in pain itself, just walking by, sweet-tempered as a
   boy.

Then Lazarus of Bethany fell sick and word
Was come. The Rabbi said he would not die.
Or something such. That's why we thought absurd
His saying two days later, staring at the sky,

"Let's to Judea." Well, you should have seen the bunch
Go taut. Was this another of his parables? Judea, mind you,
Where they think God's stones were made to crunch
A rabbi's bones, where most cheerfully they nearly slew

The only man who ever helped to set so many things to
    right.
We tried to hold him back, but nothing worked. He said
Some dark things touching daylight and some light
Ones touching sleep. Then he told us: Lazarus was dead.

I saw two things: that death was waiting like a beast
In Bethany; and death would eat our rabbi. And with that
The old, sad sickness of the world rose like a dead sun in the
    east
For me. I fell back on my toughness and I told them pat,

"Let's all go. Let's die with him." After all, if he dies
Life's as hopeless as it was before. You talk about a glum
Crew; I thought (but didn't say), let's have no pious lies
Of Pharisees on resurrection, nor glib promises, but dumb

As stones themselves go all as one with him
Into the blackness. I never was more wrong. (I take that
    back.)
Still, death collapsed before his powers once again, and he,
    as trim
As a bridegroom, handed Lazarus to life. A godly knack,

I thought, for strewing health the way a sower casts
The seed. "How does he do it?" came into my mind
And then passed on. I've known since then that no idea lasts
That evidence compels. The sovereign thing to bind

A truth with us is some surprising way of putting
    something old,
A new fruition on the same old tree. But on. Time passed.
The Passover approached, the Rabbi spoke of death in cold
Consolement as I heard it. We shaken twelve looked on
    aghast

To hear him say that he would die, as should we all,
For some vague good I didn't catch. Now? Now that death
Had cowered at his voice? And then I saw it was a stall
Back there in Bethany; the monster only waited, held its
    breath.

They took him, tried him, sold him, beat him so
Another man would plead, hung him up like meat
For kites. The rest of us had gone so many turns morale was
    low.
Our courage in exhaustion, it made a balance to retreat

Or stay with him and suicide, more Roman than a Jew
Would care to be. Before he left he said he went
To sweep a room for us past death. He said we knew
Where he was going and would follow. I'd no notion where
    he meant

And told him so. He said the way was he. I think you know
How much that braced me up when all the pebbles lay
Within the ring (as I then thought). Time seemed to slow.

I'm told, the Magdalene got John and Cephas on the run.
They thought the body stolen. Wrong again. Too neat
For thieves. The men went home. The woman, totally
    undone,
Remained behind, recalling things he meant to her, when
    who should greet

Her but the gardener. To make it short, the gardener was
    not
The gardener; the Rabbi was alive, she said. I knew the
    type.
Death is such cold and slicing steel some folks talk rot.
To keep from going mad they dream up such fulfilling tripe

As "other worlds where no one dies." That's what I thought
Of Mary's gardener. I wanted nothing more of it, or them.
The men, each time we gathered, got so overwrought
I had no stomach for it. I feared that if I stayed I'd just
    condemn

Them for their womanish self-accusations, so I stayed
Away. (My judgment never played me worse.) They said
He came to them past locks. Don't ask me how. It's not my
    trade,
This thinking hard about impossibilities like how the dead

Can turn around and not be dead. I laughed, of course,
But they were resolute. They asked me what would make
A proof to satisfy my doubts. I said, The most immediate
    source
Of this ruinous death, his wounds. If I could take

Him in my hands like any man, as well as ask my eyes,
I'd say all right, have done, the world is bright and sweet.
But now my curiosity was up. Next week I bore their
    humid sighs
Behind the fastened doors. I stood staring when he stepped
    as neat

As thinking up to me, said, "Here, in my hands, the holes.
Put your fingers there in place of the nails. Here in my side,
Make your hand the spear. Believe!" I looked at Cephas and
    our roles
Look switched to me. Time was I could hardly abide

His fawning, calling him Messiah, Lord.
Now I was there. If Cephas was a fool, the same fool I.
I saw it now: the monster sprang and ate; its victim's sword
Cut deep and wide within so that, through dying, death
    should die.

It was too good to be. And yet it was. This was the man
Who died, and here he was alive, and teaching me good
    sense.
I thought back on the healings and my short attention span,
The way the signs became more obvious for those more
    dense

Like me and, as He waited for my reply, my legs
Gave way, my eyes dissolved, I lost track of my hands,
My breathing came in gusts, and I admitted, as a blind man
    begs,
That He was God, asked His forgiveness, while the lands

Convulsed in evil's long, reptilian and dying throes.
And now, remembering it all, I lust to live again
Those subtler signs: Lazarus, the blind man, the touching
    of His clothes.
Or better yet, to not have eyed Him, just be told through
    other men.[13]

An Early Morning Communion

For several weeks Jesus appeared to his disciples and others, to James, a member of his family, to each of the disciples and then to five hundred of the brothers and sisters at one time. We have only Paul's record for these meetings and cannot describe these encounters in detail. Shortly before he left his disciples he came to them once more at the Sea of Galilee. For me this account presents the very essence of what the disciples experienced as they met the resurrected Jesus of Nazareth.[14]

Several disciples gathered at the Sea of Tiberias, the Roman name for the Sea of Galilee. The Gospel of John is very specific (as the beloved disciple often is) about those present. Simon Peter was there and with him Thomas the Twin whose story we have just heard. Nathanael from Cana-in-Galilee, the two sons of Zebedee (James and John) and two other unnamed disciples rounded out the group.

They were no longer grieving. Life had come together for them, but they had not yet realized the full significance of what they had experienced. The world-shattering meaning of Jesus' rising from the dead had not occurred to them. They were alive and whole, but they didn't see how much the whole world needed to hear and experience the hope and transformation that had transformed them. They had not yet grasped the necessity of sharing what they had experienced.

A fishing expedition can be very healing, but it is not exactly the activity to be expected by people who had been rescued from utter despair by the most important event in history. Late in the afternoon Peter announced to the group that he was going fishing, and the others, most of them probably Galilean fisherfolk, replied that they would go with him. They wasted no time in getting ready their tackle and launching the boat. Throughout the night they cast out their nets and they caught nothing, nothing. I have always marveled at the persistence and dedication of fishermen. They get up in the middle of the night to fish at the best time, travel hundreds of miles and never seem to get discouraged. I have often thought how alive and vital Christianity would be if the ordinary Christian had the self-sacrificing devotion of the run-of-the-mill fisherman.

Dawn was already breaking, and the first rays of the sun were beginning to reveal the superb beauty of the Sea of Galilee and the timbered hills around it. Jesus stood alone on the empty beach. The fishermen were heading back toward the shore. They saw a man standing there, but did not recognize that it was Jesus. He called out to them: "Hey there, you lads, have you caught anything?" How important to hear the natural, common, ordinary way that the risen Jesus spoke to his friends. His manner had nothing stilted about it. We also need to remember that these were young men; the Greek can mean nothing else. Jesus was in his very early thirties according to incarnational time. Most of his companions were about his age. None were older than their late thirties and one, perhaps, in his early twenties. Speaking as one in my late sixties, I know that I have learned much in the last twenty-five years, but I have also realized that there is a dedication, energy and power in young men and women touched by the risen Jesus that older people often do not have. Would Christianity have spread like a mountain fire over the ancient world had most of Jesus' disciples been in their sixties?

As a group the young men called back: "No." To their straightforward and discouraged reply Jesus shouted back: "Shoot the net to the starboard, and you will make a catch." Jesus knew fishing and fishermen. There was no particular reason not to make one more try after fishing all night. Out went the net. They began to haul it in and they were struck with terror. They could not even haul in all the fish the net enclosed.

John was the first to make the connection. He remembered the catch of fish when they first met Jesus, the haul which touched Peter so deeply. John spoke softly to Peter: "It is the Lord." This statement was all that Simon Peter needed to come to his senses. Impulsive, action-oriented Peter tucked his outer garment into his belt and threw himself into the water and swam to shore. The shore drops off quickly into deep water. The other disciples brought the boat to land, towing the net full of fish behind them. They were only about a hundred yards from shore.

The Fourth Gospel seldom refers to John by name, but rather as the beloved disciple or the disciple whom Jesus loved. I am much touched by this practice. Each of us is indeed the beloved disciple. The more we need him, the more he loves us, the

First of all, the risen Jesus' meeting with his friends tells us in the most striking way possible that there is more to reality than just energy and mass. Spirit is real as well and has ultimate significance. We human beings share in the reality of spirit as well as of matter just as Jesus did. We are both body and spirit, matter and soul; both were created by God and both are good. We need both in order to come to our fulfillment as amphibious human beings. The resurrection speaks to the essential unity of the physical and spiritual in our universe.

This physical body of ours can die and disintegrate, and yet a part of us continues on and can rise in a new form. We have the potential of continued life just as a dying redwood seed can give birth to a gigantic tree. Human beings had dreamed of this possibility, had hoped for it, but in the resurrection the imperishability and the transformation potential of the human being were revealed before many witnesses. Those who killed Jesus did not destroy him. There was something more to him than just a body, and there is something more to us than our physicality. How differently we look at life as the resurrection of Jesus raises and expands our horizons and our consciousness. We have an eternal destiny whether we like it or not. This can be either good news or bad news.

What good would eternal life be, life that continues forever beyond the grave, if the world on the other side is simply a continuation of this one? We would then be immersed forever in a realm of existence in which evil and ugliness, power and selfishness, hostility and destructiveness were ultimate factors. If eternal life were to be a continuation of the suffering and tragedy, the cruelty and sorrow, the futility and bitterness that so many in our world know, then it would be far better just to cease to exist. Under those circumstances death and extinction would be a blessed relief.

But the resurrection of Jesus tells us that evil has been conquered, that it is not part of the ultimate nature of things, that it is derivative and not on an equal footing with the loving God. The resurrection is the showing forth in the arena of the world that God wins, goodness wins, love conquers. The best human being was confronted by the hatred, greed and bigotry of the world. The forces of self-centeredness and evil condemned Jesus of Nazareth, judged him, crucified him; they watched and mocked him as he died. They appeared to be victorious, but God raised Jesus from the dead. The risen Jesus demonstrated the victory of what he embodied—love, meaning, hope, joy, peace, transformation, never-ending growth.

As we have already pointed out it is impossible for us to understand why evil exists and has such power. The resurrection declares that evil will not always triumph as it does so often now. In the end we can enter God's Kingdom and find continuing new life; this Kingdom will eventually come upon our earth as in heaven, but we do not need to wait for this. We can start now on the path toward new and fuller life which is manifested in the risen Jesus. In the concluding chapter I shall give several different ways by which we can enter now upon this new life. We need not be under the domination of evil. We can be free of its befouling control. The risen Christ is available now and can free us from that which seeks to destroy us.

The most difficult part of the resurrection message for me to believe is that God in Christ did all this for us long before we did anything worthy of this kind of love. Christ died, rose again and comes to us now not because we are worthy of God, but *simply because God loves us as we are.* God is seeking us out as Jesus picked out his disciples and friends and then sought them out after his resurrection to bring them back to life. The greater our need, the greater God's effort to seek us who are like the prodigal, the elder brother and the straying sheep. The resurrection reveals the loving and seeking God who would find us and help us achieve the deepest and most lasting desires of our being. What greater gift could we receive? We need simply to cease running away and receive the grace upon grace that the risen Lord holds in his hands for us.

There are three more acts in our drama and now we turn to these. Through them the resurrection is universalized and made available to all.

7.

Ascension: Parting Without Sorrow

Some days or weeks after Easter Sunday, there was a great change in the way Jesus appeared to his friends and followers. Mark does not speak of this change. In John's account of the resurrection Jesus spoke to Mary Magdalene in the garden and referred to his ascending to the Father in the present tense. There is no other reference to ascension in his Gospel. The final words of Matthew's Gospel speak of Jesus gathering his disciples together on a mountain in Galilee and giving them a commission to preach the Gospel all over the world. He also gave them authority on earth and in heaven. His physical departure is only inferred. Luke, however, clearly differentiates the resurrection, the departure of Jesus from his disciples, and his return in a new form in the Holy Spirit.

Undoubtedly these events were closely related. We are dealing with the holy in its most numinous form, and it is difficult to clearly differentiate these three aspects of Jesus' victory over death and evil. John concluded his Gospel with Jesus coming to his disciples, breathing on them, and giving them the Holy Spirit; the same gift is inferred again in the final passage of Matthew. For some of those who experienced a meeting with the risen Jesus the experience gave them hope and conviction in Jesus' victory. For some the meeting contained a quality of finality and farewell. For others the experience was one of receiving a new spiritual energy. For others all three meanings were united in one overwhelming experience. Still others experienced these three meanings as separate consecutive experiences. The Church has followed the separation of these three experiences as recorded in Luke as it has developed a liturgical practice and dogmatic tradition.

The Church separated the final encounters with Jesus into three different events: Jesus' rising from death speaks to his victory over death and affirms the divine meaning of his life; the ascension of Jesus speaks to the fact that his bodily appearances ceased and asserts the cosmic, incarnational aspect of Jesus as well as the divinization of the human carried back into the spiritual domain; the gift of the Holy Spirit at Pentecost tells of a new kind of presence of Jesus within his followers given to empower them to live out their destiny in a hostile world.

There was a period in my ministry when I was embarrassed by the feast of the Ascension. The Church treated it as one of the great days of the Christian year. On the one hand in one description Luke pictured the event in a way that made very little sense to me. The same picture is portrayed in much religious art: Jesus stepped onto a cloud and was whisked away up there into the sky, into heaven. The picture seemed ridiculous, like the ending of a naive, old-fashioned, sentimental novel. After all, which way is up? Evidently the Russian cosmonauts shared the view that heaven was supposed to be up there; they reassured their Marxist government that they did not find God or heaven on their journey into space. On the other hand Ascension Day is ranked along with Christmas, Pentecost, Easter and All Saints Day as one of the great days of the Church year.

One value of the liturgical year is that when we follow that year it forces us to deal with the great mysteries of the Christian faith. I began to ponder the account given in Luke and meditate over it. Out of the depth of this reflection I realized that there was a religious significance of the greatest value to the experience Luke describes. We do not have to link ourselves with biblical literalists who expect Jesus to return momentarily on the same kind of cloud on which he supposedly departed. We don't have to go off on a mountain to stand gazing into the heavens awaiting his return.

What actually happened to the disciples? And why is that great experience described as the ascension still of abiding and crucial importance to us today? So often our language is inadequate when we try to tell people what has happened to us.

Atomic physicists can only describe what they experience in the heart of the atom in algebraic formulas. Great art is required to give a hint of a glorious sunset over the cliff at the seashore. Great poetry alone can express the full depth of human love. Our difficulties in communication are particularly marked when we try to tell others of transforming religious experiences. In *Doors of Perception* Aldous Huxley has pointed out that most European languages are very poor in words relating to spiritual experience. If the other person has had a numinous experience we can begin to communicate, but if our experience is unknown to the other, then sharing becomes extremely difficult. If the ascension was a unique experiential *fact*, then it would have been dreadfully difficult to communicate.

In addition to these difficulties, we describe our experiences in terms of the frame of reference or the world view of which we are a part. Many different world views have existed through the ages and even today. In the time of Jesus of Nazareth, when people were observed to be acting in a completely irrational or uncharacteristic way, these people were described as demon possessed: one or more demons had gotten hold of their inner being. Now we describe this weird behavior as insanity or mental derangement, or possession by autonomous psychological trauma *or* by a psychic or spiritual reality taking over the conscious personality. Whether we call that reality a demon or an autonomous complex makes little difference if we understand that both terms refer to the same reality. A negative spiritual reality is most certainly involved in most cases of depression, anxiety and other psychological disturbances.

In the time of the evangelists they saw the sun and the stars go around the earth and they believed that the earth was the center of the universe; everything went around it. We now realize that lots of things are going around, including the earth. We describe the same experience, but we use different language. Similarly, if we return home to be confronted with a house in chaos, the drawers pulled out and the contents strewed about the floor, we could infer that a thief has been there. However, if there is a two year old in the house we are more likely to attribute the disorder to the child.

The disciples expressed the overwhelming numinous experience of being with the physical, risen Jesus for the last time in the only way available to them. The experience overwhelmed them. The King of Kings was going home to his own Kingdom. A blaze of ineffable glory and he was with them no more. Let us put ourselves back into the world and experience of that time. These people lived in a relatively simple universe. At the center was the earth, saucer-like; inverted over it was the sky, like a huge bowl. On top of the bowl was heaven. They also believed that souls were a kind of substance like an invisible gas. This substance departed from the body at death. The purer souls, like a rarer gas, went up quickly through the skies to heaven; impurer and blemished souls rose only a little way to one of the lesser heavens, and remained flitting about the earth annoying people or (misfortune of misfortunes) sank through the earth into hell itself. Many of the ancients believed that there were many degrees of heaven and that people received their just deserts by going to the first, seventh or tenth heaven depending on the purity of their souls. When the disciples were separated *physically* from their risen Lord in incandescent magnificence, how could they have explained it other than that Jesus had ascended into heaven?

We in our quite different time might have described the same experience as his breaking through into another dimension of reality, or as the door between the worlds being flung open, bathing us with heaven's brilliance. The same experience, but different descriptions depending upon our world view. Those who don't believe in anything but the physical simply dismiss the resurrection and the ascension of Jesus as nonsense because they have no place for the experience. Someone very close to me once said: "Morton, if I had a world view which allowed it I would be religious, because I have tremendous religious experiences. But since there is no place in my universe for them I pay no attention to them."

Luke gave us two descriptions of what happened to the disciples in this critical experience of joyous separation: one at the end of his Gospel, the other at the beginning of the second and continuing volume about Jesus and Christianity, the Acts of the Apostles. Luke's Gospel concludes with these words: "Jesus led them out to a spot near Bethany and blessed them with uplifted hands; in the act of blessing he was separated from them and they returned to Jerusalem with great joy, and spent all their time in the temple glorifying God." You will note that in this account there is no mention of clouds or ascending. We find these details in Luke's other version. Luke described the same experience in two different ways. In Acts Luke wrote that Jesus appeared for forty days after his resurrection, confirming their experience of his resurrectedness and teaching them about the Kingdom of God. Then Jesus met them one final time and spoke of the gift of the Holy Spirit soon to be poured out upon them. They still did not understand the full significance of his preaching and asked when Israel would come into its own sovereignty. Jesus told them directly not to worry about dates and times.

"When he had said this, as they watched, he was lifted up, and a cloud took him out of their sight. While they were gazing intently into heaven while he was leaving, there suddenly beside them stood two men in white who said: 'Men of Galilee, why are you standing there gazing into heaven? This Jesus, who has been taken up from you into heaven, will come in the same way as you saw him go into heaven.' Then they returned from the mount of Olivet, which is only a sabbath day's journey from Jerusalem. . . . Entering the city they went to an upstairs room where they were staying. . . . All of these were constantly at prayer together and with them were a group of women, including Mary, the Mother of Jesus, and others of his family."

The "rising up" of Jesus is secondary to a magnificent parting. Jesus was also hid by a cloud on the mount of transfiguration where in the presence of God Jesus was transformed. The pillar of cloud was one manifestation of God in the Old Testament. James Kirsch has written in depth about the significance of the cloud as divine manifestation in his book, *The Reluctant Prophet*.[1] These disciples had experienced the reality of the divine in a remarkable way.

The strangest part of Luke's account of this parting is not the description that the beholders gave of their experience, but their reaction to it. We have heard this story so many times that we fail to realize its unusualness. Would we expect his disciples to part with their Lord with great joy? Would we have expected them to take leave of the one they had loved more than life itself and proceed to Jerusalem with *great joy* and to remain in joyous prayer and praise after that? Had I been making up this story I would probably have written: "And leaving the mount of Olivet with their eyes running with tears they said to one another, 'It was a wonderful experience while it lasted. It will be lonely as we await his return. So sad, so strange the days that are no more.' Then they went back with heavy hearts and grim determination to the tasks Jesus had appointed them to do."

In the story of the translation or ascension of Elijah, we find the natural reaction to such a separation under quite similar circumstances. As Elijah was carried away into heaven in the chariot of fire, Elisha, who was his disciple, companion and friend, cried out, "My father, my father, the chariots of Israel and the horsemen thereof." Then in a typical Hebrew expression of profound grief, he ripped his clothes apart.

Jesus of Nazareth is the only great hero in history for whom no elegy has ever been written and for whom no dirge was ever sung. Indeed this lack of sadness is the key to understanding the significance of this parting of the Lord from the disciples. The disciples had lost nothing. The early Christians never spoke of remembering Jesus. He was for them a present reality; he was continually with them.

The continuing resurrection experiences had as one of their purposes the preparing of the disciples for separation from the physical Jesus. In many of Jesus' appearances he was known as much by spiritual intuition as by ordinary sense experience. In the garden, Mary recognized Jesus not by sight at first, but by the inflection of his voice. On the road to Emmaus the disciples reported that their hearts had burned within them, but they did not recognize him until he broke bread before them. Experiences like these trained the followers of Jesus to know him by spiritual perception.

The resurrected Jesus appeared suddenly and then disappeared in the same way. Perhaps their risen Lord was trying to train them to be constantly aware of his presence, to be spiritually on tiptoe. These strange comings and goings fostered this kind of awareness. Since they never knew when he would be present with them or in their midst they came to think of his presence in every conversation, at every meeting with a friend, accompanying every thought. They became constantly open to his presence. They came to rely on their spiritual apprehension of him as well as their physical perception. These meetings lasted only until his followers were convinced of his resurrection and of his never-failing presence. Finally he parted from them with a promise that something more was to be given them.

The early Christians looked upon the parting not as a loss, but as the final confirmation of his victory, the affirmation of the incarnation. That which had come physically into the world now departed, taking humanness into heaven and divinizing it. The incarnate Son of God was returning to the Godhead, from which he came. It was the final and complete vindication of everything that he had lived, taught and died for. From now on his presence would not be localized in one spot or time. His life assumed a cosmic nature. He became infinitely available, just like God. The numinous parting with Jesus did not mean that their friend and master was gone, but that he would now be with them even when they were scattered over the face of the earth; he was now always with them. Paul wrote: "What can separate us from the love of Christ? . . . For I am convinced that nothing in death or life, in the cosmic realm of spirits, or spiritual powers both good and evil, or in the natural human world as it is or as it shall become, in the rising and setting of the stars, or in anything else in all creation, can separate us from the love of God in Christ Jesus our Lord" (Rom 8:35–39).

Had some modern person stood with the disciples at the joyful parting with the risen Jesus, the experience would probably have been expressed in words like those of Howard Chandler Robbins:

And have the bright immensities
    Received our risen Lord,
Where light-years frame the Pleiades
    And point Orion's sword?
Do flaming suns his footsteps trace
    Through corridors sublime,
The Lord of interstellar space
    And conqueror of time?

The heaven that hides him from our sight
  Knows neither near nor far:
An altar candle sheds its light
  As surely as a star;
And where his loving people meet
  To share the gift divine,
There stands he with unhurrying feet;
  There heavenly splendors shine.[2]

An Essential Part of the Drama

Sometimes the action of a drama may seem irrelevant until we come to the end of the play. When the glorious parting of the risen Jesus is separated entirely from the rest of the divine drama it makes little sense. When this act of the play is understood in the progression of incarnation, death, resurrection and the pouring forth of divine gifts at Pentecost, the feast day which is inadequately described as the Ascension is essential to the action.

First of all, as the early Christians went out to preach the Gospel, they preached the good news of the resurrection of Jesus. The question would have inevitably risen from those who listened to them: And where is Jesus now if he has risen from the dead? There are times when I wish that he might be around so I could make a trip and consult him, but God was far wiser; we need to learn to depend not only on our physical senses, but on the other senses of our souls, which are not bound to the earth. Without the divine parting, the cosmic return, Christ would have been a world power and Christianity would have been a power game; our freedom would have been taken from us. God loves us too much to take our freedom from us.

This final magnificent experience of the physical risen Jesus also taught his followers to develop their spiritual lives. The risen Jesus had now assumed a cosmic stature and was available as people came to Eucharist, turned in quiet to commune with him on the other side of silence, or called out in sickness, need or persecution to One who saved. They were then open to the spontaneous divine manifestations that God continually gives us in the Pentecostal experience, in dreams, in revelations, visions and

healings. This experience prepared them for his continual pres-
entness with them.

In *The Answer to Job* Jung wrote that he had the courage to
take up the subject of the dogma of the assumption of the Virgin
Mary because "I consider [it] to be the most important religious
event since the Reformation."[3] Jung's enthusiasm stems from his
understanding of the assumption as the event which united earth
and heaven, bringing the physical and spiritual into intimate
communion. Unfortunately, the Christian Church affirmed the
Creed of Chalcedon (in which it is stated with utter clarity that
Jesus was both human and divine and that the two can not be separated or divided) but did not live it out. So much of Christianity
has emphasized only the divine aspect of Jesus, the Christ, that
we have a tendency to forget and neglect his humanness. When
this happens we do not understand that in the divine return of the
risen Jesus the meeting and mingling of the divine and human is
affirmed as much as in the incarnation or the assumption. Had
Jung understood the importance of the ascension of Jesus he
could have been as enthusiastic about this event as he was about
the assumption. Both speak of the interrelation of the spiritual
and the physical, the earthly and heavenly. The ascension of Jesus, even more than the assumption of Mary, accomplished this
union.

Indeed the ascension of Jesus, the overwhelming experience
of the divine return, is the inevitable result of the incarnation and
the necessary preparation for the outpouring of the divine gifts at
Pentecost. This final experience of the risen Jesus was for the disciples a door between the worlds and reaffirmed their belief that
Jesus was God in the flesh. It also prepared them for another ineffable experience which they described as the coming of the
Holy Spirit.

8.

A New Incarnation—
The Coming of the Holy Spirit

In the past eighty years the importance of Pentecost and the outpouring of the Holy Spirit have been much more appreciated in
Western Christendom. For many years Western Christianity had
been almost binitarian in practice; in actual devotional life God
the Creator and Jesus the Redeemer were invoked, but seldom
the third person of the Trinity, the Holy Spirit. The Greek Orthodox Church, however, maintained emphasis on the Paraclete
(John's designation for the Holy Spirit). At the turn of the twen-
tieth century, Pentecostal churches were founded and grew rap-
idly because many people discovered that there was a life and
power available to Christians that many of the mainline Christian
churches had forgotten. In the past thirty years this understanding spread to many Protestant denominations. Early in his pa-
pacy, in *Humanae Salutis*, Pope John XXIII called for people to
pray that the Holy Spirit might renew the Church and so prepare
for the Second Vatican Council. The charismatic movement em-
phasizing the reality and empowerment of the Holy Spirit then
began to spread like wildfire in a renewed Roman Catholic
Church.[1]

So much has been written in recent times about the Holy
Spirit that it may seem presumptuous to devote one short chapter
to the subject. A large portion of my writing has been devoted to
studying the effects of the Holy Spirit as it touches and transforms the lives of human beings throughout the ages right up to

the present time.[2] The basic idea of this renewal movement is that God still acts in the lives of Christians today as the Holy Spirit did among the Christians described in the Acts of the Apostles and the letters of Paul. From the point of view of the first Christians the action of God in our world did not cease with the ascension. After this event the disciples and apostles were given a new spiritual life and energy, a new spiritual companion who operated within and through them and made different people of them.

Something of a momentous nature happened at Pentecost to the followers of Jesus. In the New Testament the importance of Pentecost is mainly delineated in Luke's two-volume work, The Gospel According to Luke and the Acts of the Apostles. At Pentecost the apostles came to the *realization* that the Holy Spirit had been given them, or they at least experienced it as given in a new way. This experience might be compared with the experience of Jesus at his baptism and temptation where he came to full consciousness of his person and destiny. Christians open to the gift were given the very Spirit of God, who had been revealed to them in the life, death, resurrection and ascension of Jesus. This spiritual reality, the very spirit that Jesus embodied, was now incarnated in a lesser measure in dedicated Christian believers. Justin Martyr expressed it well and succinctly in these words: "Jesus became what we are in order that we might become what he is."

Mark's Gospel does not speak of this event. After careful consideration of all the evidence I am convinced that we do not have the final pages of Mark's Gospel. Even if we did I doubt if he would have described anything to do with Pentecost. This was not his purpose. As we have already indicated his goal was to preserve the facts of Jesus' life. He probably wrote his work living in a resurrection-ascension-Spirit-filled time. He was so much a part of it that in his hurried, almost breathless, presentation he did not reflect upon all that had been given him.

Matthew writes little about the giving of the Holy Spirit. That he knew of the action of the Spirit is clear when he quotes Jesus' saying that when they were arrested they need not worry about what they should say because "it will be the Spirit of your Father speaking in you" (10:20). In the concluding scene of Matthew's Gospel Jesus gathers his disciples around him and passes his authority on to them, telling them to baptize "in the name of the Father and the Son and the Holy Spirit, and to teach them to observe all that I commanded you" (28:20). Matthew's interest was not so much in the life of the Church in the apostolic age as in providing a new law and teaching and in preserving that tradition for future generations.

The Gospel According to John likewise ends with the actual ministry of Jesus of Nazareth. However that Gospel places great emphasis on the *Paraclete* who cannot come until Jesus leaves and who will be the defender of the persecuted, the empowerer, the giver of wisdom and new life. In John 20:19ff Jesus appears to the disciples, greets them, and shows them his hands and feet. He then tells them: "As the Father has sent me, so I send you." Then he breathes on them and says: "Receive the Holy Spirit," and goes on to give them authority to forgive or to retain human sins. This tradition is certainly parallel to that of Luke. John's purpose was to record the saving life-death-resurrection of Jesus rather than to record the effect of the gift of the Holy Spirit upon Jesus' followers.[3]

Luke has two purposes in writing. First he provided a connected narrative about the events occurring around Jesus of Nazareth. Then he gave a history of what happened in the life of the Church as the Holy Spirit was poured out on Jesus' followers. This second work demonstrated the continued presence and power of Jesus' Spirit in the life of the Church. Acts begins with a description of the ascension. It goes on to tell of a powerful experience in which the disciples are filled with something they had not known before. The first action of Peter after receiving this gift is to preach with such persuasion that many were converted. The next recorded activity of the apostles is the healing of the lame man at the Beautiful Gate of the temple by Peter and John. It is clear from these descriptions that Jesus' power had passed on to the apostles. The Church continued to grow and the same Holy Spirit was manifested by Stephen. As they were about to stone him the Holy Spirit revealed to him Jesus standing at God's right hand. Then the risen and still present Jesus of Nazareth came to Paul and converted him. He was filled with the Holy

Spirit and became one of the most important leaders of the nascent Church.

Paul's letters describe the action of the Holy Spirit in providing the presence and power of the risen Jesus in terms quite similar to those in descriptions of event after event in Acts. In several places Paul describes the various powers or gifts of the Holy Spirit. Luke's second volume, in fact, might be called a history of the Holy Spirit. The Christ-life was growing continually as more and more people became Christians and were filled with the Holy Spirit. The fire that was lighted on Pentecost was consuming more and more of the world.

Luke described the original experience of fire in these words: "On the day of Pentecost all of them were together in one place, the disciples, the women who had been close to Jesus and others. Suddenly from heaven came the sound of powerful wind; this wind filled the entire house where they were sitting. And there appeared to them tongues like flames of fire that rested upon each of those there. And they were filled with the Holy Spirit and began to speak in other tongues that the Spirit gave them the power to speak." It is much easier to make sense of this experience when we realize that modern men and women testify to similar experiences that have remade their lives.

Here is the statement of a very normal person known to me who had such an experience in a prayer group in the church of which I was rector.

> I was kneeling as four others prayed for me. They put their hands on my head and on my shoulders. . . . The prayer was simple—a request for a greater flow of Spirit within me. I was open and expectant. And then it happened! . . . It was like a baptism. I felt that I was going down, then coming up. Or, the feeling was like draining out, and refilling. It was all an inner thing—down and then up. As I "came up" I spoke in tongues and interpreted.
>
> Besides the tongues and the interpretation, my hands felt full, as if there was much to pass through them—and on out. I was filled with tremendous joy. Laughter came easily. It was tremendously exhilarating, and it was not easy to sleep that night! The next day was much the same. I felt different,

I was different. . . . Passages of Scripture I had read before
and did not understand were opened in this [the experience of
tongues] and many other areas.[4]

The Meaning of Pentecost

This Christian experience of being filled with the Spirit of
God is intimately linked to the loving, suffering, risen Jesus of
Nazareth. Without the resurrection of Jesus this experience
makes no sense. In the same way Jesus' rising from the dead is
more than a victory that occurred once. Resurrection came to
fruition in the giving of the Holy Spirit; in a very real way Jesus'
victory was imparted to people so that they could share in it.

What happened to those in the Bible who received this spiritual reality? People have much the same experiences today. First
of all they were washed free of many of the hindrances of their
broken natures. They were forgiven. This opened up wells of life
within them. Receiving the Spirit was not once for all; however,
when they knew that such a reality was available they could turn
again and again to it and be regenerated bit by bit. The gift of the
Holy Spirit made them open to participate in its life. The early
Christians were given unbelievable courage and strength as they
faced persecution, torture and death. The prison doctor who
watched Dietrich Bonhoeffer go to his death under the Nazis on
April 9, 1945 reported that he had never seen anyone die so entirely submissive to the will of God. The early Christians were
given ghostly strength. In addition the courage that Christians
expressed as they were thrown to the lions transformed scornful
opponents of Christianity into sympathetic onlookers and finally
drew them into the fold. The blood of the martyrs was the seed
of the Church.

The disciples were given new powers and abilities. The
Spirit of Christ released or created abilities within them that they
did not have before. The original band of Galilean peasants confronted the world of power and learning and eventually won both
over to their faith in the risen Jesus Christ. The strange outpouring of the gifts of the Spirit on the disciples is described by Paul
in several passages and described in individual instances in the

historical narrative of Acts. The spiritual domain of God and of the risen Jesus was opened to them in a new way. They were given revelations and divine guidance. Like Jesus they had the power to heal the physically and mentally ill as well as the demon-possessed. They could understand the spiritual significance of events and what influences operated within people. Their natural extrasensory perceptions were heightened, and then many of them spoke prophetically as if God were speaking through them. Some of them spoke in tongues.

In Jesus of Nazareth love and power met and mingled. In many of the early Christians the same love and power were observable. They claimed that it was the Spirit and presence of Jesus which gave it to them. A Zen Buddhist monk once remarked: "We think that there is something in Christianity, but we don't think that Christians know what it is." A friend of mine commented on this statement by remarking to me: "After twenty-five years in the Christian ministry, and fifteen of those spent in denominational service and ecumenical affairs, I would have to concede that the Buddhist monk has pretty big substantiation for his remark." I find myself wondering, of course, what the Zen Buddhist monk thought there might be in Christianity. My guess is that he had reference to a kind of spiritual power.

This experience of receiving the Holy Spirit can come to some people as it did to the apostles at Pentecost as a rushing mighty wind and like tongues of fire that sear the heart. Such people have to remain open to that Spirit or they can become spiritually dead. To other people the Holy Spirit may come much more gradually, imperceptibly changing them until they are really quite different. How important to realize that God treats each of us as individuals, giving us the Spirit in the way most meaningful, creative and congenial to us. The purpose of the Christian Church is to bring all different kinds of people into living relationship with the reality and Spirit of the risen Jesus so that it can transform us. The goal of Christianity is to make silk purses out of sows' ears.

I do not know how the following poem came into my hand. I don't know the author. It is not great poetry, but it does give a sense of what many people have felt when they have been touched by the Spirit of the resurrected Jesus of Nazareth.

T'was battered, scarred, and the auctioneer
    thought it scarcely worth the while
To waste his time on the old violin,
    but he held it up with a smile.
"What am I bid, good people," he cried,
    "Who'll start the bidding for me?
One dollar? One dollar . . . now do I hear two?
    Two dollars . . . now who makes it three?

Three dollars once . . . three dollars twice,
    going for three . . ." But no!
From the room far back a greybearded man
    came forward and picked up the bow.
Then wiping the dust from the old violin
    and tightening up the strings
He played a melody, pure and sweet,
    as sweet as the angels sing.

The music ceased, and the auctioneer
    with a voice that was quiet and low
Said, "What now am I bid for the old violin?"
    As he held it aloft with its bow.
"One thousand?" said he. "Two thousand?
    and now two thousand and who makes it three?
Three thousand once, three thousand twice . . .
    and going and gone" said he.

The people cheered, but some of them cried,
    "We don't quite understand . . .
What changed its worth?" Swift came the reply,
    "The touch of a master's hand."
And many a man with life out of tune,
    all battered and torn with sin
Is auctioned cheap to a thoughtless crowd
    much like the old violin.

A mess of pottage, a glass of wine,
    a game, and he travels on
He is going once, he is going twice,
    he is going and almost gone.
But the Master comes and the foolish crowd
    never can quite understand
The worth of a soul, that change that was wrought
    by the touch of the Master's hand.

People who have experienced the Spirit have felt like useless earthen vessels filled with gold and precious stones, like broken cisterns made whole and filled with streams of living water, like old violins touched by the master's hand. Broken and tired humans, battered and used mortals, have become the dwelling place, the temple of Jesus' Spirit, and have gained incomparable worth.

In 1660 after being imprisoned in England for his religious beliefs, James Nayler was released and reconciled with the Society of Friends. Shortly after that he set out from London intending to visit his wife and children in Wakefield. On the way he was robbed, beaten and found bound in a field. Some members of the Society of Friends found him and brought him into their home where he died. About two hours before he died he spoke the following words that were taken down as he spoke them:

> There is a spirit which I feel that delights to do no evil, nor to revenge any wrong, but delights to endure all things, in hope to enjoy its own in the end. Its hope is to outlive all wrath and contention, and to weary out all exaltation and cruelty, or whatever is of a nature contrary to itself. It sees to the end of all temptations. As it bears no evil in itself, so it conceives none in thoughts to any other. If it be betrayed, it bears it, for its ground and spring is the mercies and forgiveness of God. Its crown is meekness, its life is everlasting love unfeigned; and takes its kingdom with entreaty and not with contention, and keeps it by lowliness of mind. In God alone it can rejoice, though none else regard it, or can own its life. It's conceived in sorrow, and brought forth without any to pity it, nor doth it murmur at grief and oppression. It never rejoiceth but through sufferings; for with the world's joy it is murdered. I found it alone, being forsaken. I have fellowship therein with them who lived in dens and desolate places in the earth, who through death obtained this resurrection and eternal holy life.

These words could have been written to describe the suffering and victory of Jesus of Nazareth. The Spirit of which Nayler spoke was the Spirit of the risen Jesus.

This kind of experience happens in our day as well. An attractive and intelligent married woman recently shared an experience that she had as a child, an experience uncovered after work in psychotherapy. I had asked a group to share their most important religious experience with me so I could share these with the group. I put the story in her words and changed details for obvious reasons.

> When I was nine years old, I was taken and very brutally attacked by three men for several hours. My whole inner being was begging to die in order to escape the physical pain I was experiencing. At one point I was in a semi-conscious state and I could hear the men talking about how to dispose of my "dead" body. I could not speak or move to tell them I wasn't dead yet. I felt my body in the process of dying and was glad that I could finally escape the pain.
>
> Then I became aware that I could choose whether I lived or died. When I realized I had a choice, I couldn't make up my mind. I had strong feelings for both life and death. A voice was telling me that time was running out and I had to make a decision soon! Or it would be too late—I would be irreversibly dead.
>
> As I considered never seeing my "mommy" and "daddy" again—their grief over my disappearance—their sadness over not having me with them—I chose to live.
>
> After I made that choice I heard a voice telling me to move my body so the men would know I was still alive. I could not move even a muscle on my own and then Jesus appeared to me standing by my right foot (I was on the ground). He reached down and moved my legs and one of the men saw me move and took compassion on me. The man wrapped me in a blanket, took me to his dwelling, cleaned me up and took me home.
>
> I did not see Jesus' face. I just knew who he was. I say he—what I saw was a large, gentle white figure. There were no words—just an atmosphere of deep, deep caring and a wave of peace filled my body. All my pain and bruises and cuts felt healed.

One of the central mysteries of the Christian faith is the relation of the various persons of the Godhead and particularly the relation of the risen Jesus and the Holy Spirit. In this adult's story about her childhood experience we find the Spirit prompting her both to have the courage to live and to move her body. This kind of experience is often associated with the action of the Holy Spirit. Then came the critical and unsought experience of the luminous, victorious Jesus standing by her and moving her leg. The resurrected Jesus Christ was also experienced as a living, still available, present, saving reality.

The essential meaning of the experience of the Holy Spirit, the giving of the Paraclete (advocate, defender, redeemer), is the continued availability of the risen Jesus of Nazareth. This can be experienced as a Spirit within us, of which James Nayler spoke. The child also first experienced help in this way. Or the presence of Jesus, who conquered death and evil, can be known and encountered. This encounter can be transforming.

The next important question now presents itself. If such love and healing power are still available, how do we open ourselves to receive them?

9.

Response to Resurrection: Release from Oppression

When the feast was over and the bones of the fatted calf had been picked clean, was there any change in the prodigal son? He now realized the incredible love and forgiveness of his father, how much he was loved. Now it depended on him. Would he respond? Would he seek out his father's companionship and be molded by that love into the kind of person his father was? Would he seek out his brother and relate to him? Would he treat the servants in a new way? When he went out into the village and beyond would he be fair and kind to the just and the unjust? When he was discouraged would he return to his father for encouragement, enlightenment and love? The same questions could be asked of the elder brother. The same questions can be asked of us after we have really heard the resurrection story or after we have celebrated the feast of Easter. How can we continue to be vividly aware of Jesus' saving presence? How can we continue to share in his victory over evil and death? How do we respond to the divine drama so that its purpose can be completed in us, so that Jesus' birth and life and death, his resurrection and giving of himself in the Holy Spirit, were not done for us in vain?

Incomprehensible as it seems to us most of the time, this divine action was undertaken for us, to deliver us from bondage to the many things that oppress us. The word "save" has many meanings. When we are saved we are delivered from those things that keep us from our full potential as human beings; we are released and are started on the way to wholeness, healing and transformation. How do we participate in this new life, in salvation? Many different answers have been given to this question. Some of the answers have stressed that faith alone is necessary (total belief in the love expressed in Jesus' death and resurrection). Others have emphasized corporate worship; for some it is a matter of the life of prayer and contemplation and Bible study. Still others have pointed to works of love, mercy and social action as the way to fellowship with the risen Christ. These different points of view have often been in violent opposition to each other, each claiming the exclusive answer. This is not the place to solve these theological issues. However, I cannot bring these reflections on the importance of the resurrection of Jesus to a close without describing some of the most significant ways in which we can respond to this event so that Jesus' victory is still experienced as saving power in our own lives. Our response is the final act of our drama and an essential one. The treatment that follows is, of course, limited by space and only suggestive.

I have pondered and prayed and meditated over this matter of our response to resurrection for many years. I have found that many of the traditional answers were helpful, but that some of the most helpful devotional methods were not as well known. On the one hand our response to resurrection can be part of an overwhelming religious experience that totally absorbs our lives; from this point of view our answer appears quite simple. This is a valid and important way of encountering the risen Jesus. However, some people who respond in this total way can be impatient and even critical of those who come to participation in the resurrection in another way. For many of us who are trying to separate ourselves from meaningless materialism, it is helpful to try to understand the process by which we open the door of our inner being to the resurrection message and reality. This process is the subject of ascetical theology and is quite complex. However, a study of this process can give us methods by which we can open ourselves to the Christ who seeks us.

Through my own experience and my study of Christian tradition I have discovered seven separable and interlocking elements in a conscious response to the resurrection drama.[1] As I grow in the Christian life I find new ways of responding. These seven are my best expression at this present time. Alcoholics

Anonymous, which has had great success in rescuing those oppressed with addiction to alcohol, uses a twelve-step program in-
corporating many of these elements.

1. We must let the story of the resurrection break into our
consciousness and upset our unconscious participation in the ordinary world around us; we need to realize that the resurrection
is something quite extraordinary and does not fit into life as
usual.

2. Once we see the resurrection as an earth-shattering
event, we must learn all we can about this man Jesus of Nazareth;
the resurrection says that this man reveals the very grain of the
universe, its heart and center.

3. We need to learn how we can be open to Jesus' continuing presence, his availability in the Spirit. There are many different ways to take down the barriers within us which shut out
the power of the risen Jesus and his Spirit.

4. If we are to be transformed by our relationship and grow
closer to this God of love, we need to bring our lives and actions
into harmony with love. This also means that we become agents
of love in an unjust society.

5. This kind of response requires courage, for we struggle
not only against a society which ridicules but also against the
very powers of darkness that seek to prevent the victory of Love.

6. We human beings are multi-leveled creatures. Bringing
all of the depth of us into harmony with the risen Jesus cannot be
accomplished in one decision or action; it is a lifelong process and
may even extend beyond the grave.

7. We need to use our common sense and check all of what
we do against the wisdom of the Church and the world, using the
critical and rational gifts with which God has endowed us.

Revolutionary Resurrection

The first reaction of the women and the disciples to the news
of Jesus' rising was fear. Their world was turned upside down.
Even when Jesus met his disciples and fed them at the Sea of Galilee, they were afraid to acknowledge him or start up a conversation. Paul's reaction to Jesus on the Damascus road was

blindness. Meeting God face to face can be a chilling experience. The Old Testament questions whether one can survive the experience. Meeting the risen Jesus is an encounter with the numinous, the holy, God acting in the world. When we catch the depth and power and meaning of this event a chill of fear may well run up our spines. We realize that God and the spiritual world are much closer than we thought. God is interested in us and his Spirit hovers close to us and is concerned with what we are and do. For most of us whose lives are not totally centered in Jesus' Kingdom, this realization of God's closeness and power is a bit upsetting. Along with Peter we feel like saying, "Depart from me, for I am a sinful person." We can't run our lives in the same casual offhand way once we truly *believe* in Easter and the resurrection of Jesus. We are brought face to face with a loving reality that holds the whole world in caring hands. We are an unclean part of that world. We feel contrite and need to confess our failings.

In the Western world two methods of avoiding the strong message of the resurrection are frequently found. The first is very simple; we deny that there is any spiritual world and assert that God is an anthropomorphic creation of human wishful thinking. If we truly believe that our universe has no meaning and is merely the product of blind chance, then we are free to die and live as we please. The most powerful can take over the world and treat others as they wish; might makes right. At least this way of thinking can be honest and consistent.

The second way of avoiding the demanding message of Easter is to sentimentalize it. Jesus' rising from the dead is a spring festival with leaves breaking forth after the dead of winter, a butterfly emerging from a chrysalis, a tadpole from a dormant egg. These images can be used to illustrate transformation, but they do not express the radical nature of the life and death of Jesus and the gift of the Holy Spirit. Indeed they may even suggest that after death we can expect an automatic rebirth to a new and perfect life, a heaven without wrinkle or blemish. God treats us all like spoiled children no matter what we do or have done. This is the reason why going to church once a year is all that is needed; we just need to have our memories refreshed. We don't need to put ourselves out for others. We might as well get all the nice

things of this world: the Porsche, the mansion by the beach, lei-
surely cruises and the finest parties. After all we get perfect bliss
after death in a heaven that meets all our desires. This attitude is
further from real Christianity and the risen Jesus than the utter
denial of thoroughgoing materialism. Unfortunately many people who do not understand the Gospel really think that Christianity proposes something like this and makes no demands upon
us. This is a very cheap Gospel that has little attraction or power.

Resurrection and Oppression

A recent book by Lewis Swedes is entitled *How Can It Be All
Right When Everything Is All Wrong?* For many people life is a real
struggle. We can be oppressed in so many different ways. For
suffering people the Gospel is not cheap; it tells them that there is
hope and that life can be more than they are experiencing. Jesus
lived among the poor, and real Christianity reaches out to those
ground down by poverty and oppression and torture. The ever
present risen Christ can give hope to help us struggle through
these difficulties as well as the wisdom to change the governments and the systems that use people and rob them of their humanity. For suffering, struggling people the Gospel is not
frightening; it is only good news. Mother Teresa, Martin Luther
King, Jr., William Wilberforce, St. Francis and many others
have brought the transforming good news to these people.
    There are times when life falls in upon us. We are struck
down by sickness or the illness of a loved one, we are torn apart
by the death of a child, or we face our own death. I have nothing
to bring to such people if I do not bring the risen Christ, who
reaches out to them with outstretched arms and with promises
that extend beyond this world. Sometimes we are betrayed or
condemned unjustly; life turns sour and we feel hopeless. St.
Catherine of Genoa and her followers had a ministry to those
condemned to die, and she herself lived and worked in a hospital.
Most of those who labor effectively among the suffering and oppressed have been touched by the victory of the risen One. Without the sustaining power of Jesus' Spirit it is nearly impossible to
bear all this pain. Physicians who deal continually with human

misery are often deeply damaged by it unless they have a vital religious point of view.

Even when we human beings are free from outer oppression we can be oppressed psychologically by fear, by meaninglessness, by cowardice or by the inner darkness which attacks and destroys. Indeed those who live comfortable exterior lives are more vulnerable to inner oppression. There is seldom any way to escape spiritual growth. These kinds of inner oppression can create untold suffering and immobilize us; they can destroy the very structure of our psyches so that we cannot function at all. Recent surveys of the homeless destitute in the United States show that many of these people were turned out of hospitals for the mentally ill and left to fend for themselves. Between Christian confession and contrition and psychological self-flagellation there is a great gulf fixed. In contrition we acknowledge our failings, faults and evil in the presence of love that has overcome them; in despair we look at these same aspects of ourselves in a void, in the darkness, hearing only the mocking condemnation of the powers of evil. Alcoholics Anonymous is an example of an organization that succeeds because it provides for genuine contrition in the presence of a saving God and an accepting community.

There are physical, social, psychological and spiritual causes for mental distress. However, whatever the causes, a sense of hopelessness is part of nearly all psychological illness. As my psychologist friend, Dr. Andrew Canale, has pointed out in a forthcoming book on depression, there is a spiritual dimension in all depression. When I feel hopeless or fearful of death, self-critical or of no value, there is no ultimate answer to my inner pain other than the risen Jesus who knocks at the doorway of my soul and enters when I listen and open the door. By his love he gives me value; by his rising he takes away my existential fear; by his victory over evil he frees me from the attacks of the evil one. So much of our psychological malaise springs from our inability to believe that we can be loved; unfathomable love which conquered evil and death is available to us from the resurrected One. I know of no other ultimate answer to our fear, cowardice and inner darkness than the loving action of God at Easter, which rescues those who take it into themselves and then in joy share their release with others. Blessed are the oppressed, for they can respond to the risen Jesus with power and find a new life in the Kingdom *on earth and in heaven*. So important is our social response to resurrection that I asked my friend Howard Rice to write an epilogue to this book on the necessary social implications of resurrection. This is more his expertise than mine.

Knowing God Through Jesus: The Importance of Scripture

Once we have been touched by the meaning of Jesus' rising, then Jesus becomes extremely important to us. Indeed, he becomes the way, the truth, and the life. We want to know as much as we can about him and about the religion in which he was raised, about his family and his birth, his teaching, his life, his betrayal and death. All of this will be pregnant with meaning for us. Learning about Jesus means knowing the Bible. Jesus' life and teaching make sense only as we understand the Old Testament, the Scripture upon which he was raised. This book is of incomparable value in itself and is one of the great religious books of humankind. In addition, knowing this great book of Judaism is essential if we would understand the life and message of Jesus. Judaism interprets this library of Hebraic religious experience through many commentaries. Christians interpret it through the eyes of Jesus.

This sacred literature of the Old and New Testaments seems almost alive; it speaks to us in our various conditions. Many people through the ages have been nourished by this book and through it have had a living and transforming relation with the Holy Spirit, the Spirit of the risen Jesus. No person who can read and write is truly serious about being engaged with the risen Lord, who does not know, study and meditate on the biblical narrative, particularly the Gospels, Acts and the Epistles. I have studied and read through the entire Bible for more than forty years, and it still opens new vistas before my inner eye and amazes me with a wealth of new insights. This book is inexhaustible in depth and wisdom.

Knowing and understanding the entire Bible is no easy task. This book is actually a whole library of books on religious experience of different ages and of different values. The Holy Spirit seldom provides us with knowledge that we can provide for ourselves by our reading and study. Being open to the transforming power of the resurrected Jesus means knowing about him; this is one essential part of a genuine response to the Christ.

When I first began to study Christianity seriously I was struck by two parts of the story. Jesus' suffering and death spoke to my inner agony and pain and told me that here was one who knew the human lot who could understand me and bear my darkness with me. I have found it helpful to have a crucifix somewhere near to remind me when I feel sorry for myself that I am not alone. Second, when I realized that the resurrection of Jesus transformed his weak-kneed, cowardly disciples into a band of courageous and victorious men and women, I then began to hope that he might make something of my sinful and neurotic being. The first part of the history of the Church is found in Acts. Few stories have inspired me more than the continuing history of the Christian community as it struggled and failed and turned again to the risen Lord and was regenerated. We can learn so much about how humans get in the way of the Spirit and how we can be open to this transforming power as we study the life of the Church and its heroes and heroines (the saints) throughout the ages. Reading the devotional masters of the Church from Justin Martyr and Augustine to John Woolman and Ignatius of Loyola has confirmed for me the continuing transforming presence of the Christ.

The Bible study in seminary gave me an excellent intellectual knowledge of the Greek and Hebrew texts, *but it did not feed my soul*. It was only after I came to understand the depth psychology of Carl Jung and realized that symbols are more alive than ideas that the Bible began to speak to me. The Bible needs to be read with the heart and imagination *as well as* with the intellect. Reading Charles Williams, C.S. Lewis, T.S. Eliot and Dorothy Sayers' translation of Dante, I realized that the Bible spoke of this physical world, of our psychological inner being and of the spiritual world as well. Until we have an understanding of the reality of the spiritual world it is nearly impossible to hear the full range of divine music in the Bible and the tradition of the Church. All our religious ideas and experience need to be checked with this tradition before we accept them as valid.

The best approach to studying the Bible that I know is the work of Walter Wink in two books, *The Bible in Human Transformation* and *Transforming Bible Study*. Dr. Wink knows the value of a critical understanding of the Bible and at the same time knows the depth of the human psyche and how we human beings can be opened to the transforming power of the risen Lord. Few practices have been more helpful to me than entering into the stories of the resurrection as I have in Chapter 6, or spending an hour or so with one of the parables of Jesus. I have spent hundreds of hours meditating on the Lord's Prayer and the Beatitudes.[2]

The basic message of Christianity is not given in a philosophical system or in concepts, but in symbols, images, story, drama. Gustaf Aulén's book, *The Drama and the Symbols*, makes this point with power and scholarship.[3] In Willa Cather's novel *Death Comes for the Archbishop*, Bishop Latour is rescued from his own darkness by ministering to an enslaved Mexican peon. Then he reflects on the importance of images in the worship of these people: "The tapers, the image of the Virgin, the figures of the saints, the Cross that took away indignity from suffering and made pain and poverty a means of fellowship with Christ. . . . Ah, for one who cannot read—or think—the Image, the physical form of love."[4] I would only add that for those who can read and think, these images still open us to the power of the risen One.

In the late 1960's David Stanley published a study of the use of the imagination in biblical study entitled "Contemplation of the Gospels, Ignatius Loyola, and the Contemporary Christian." He stated that following the ascension and Pentecost, Jesus actually is "more dynamically present in the world than ever he was when he walked the hills of Galilee." He also stated that Jesus' earthly history contains concealed within it a new and enduring reality. He then suggests that contemplating this earthly history can be a way of relating at the present time to the present reality of the risen Lord. This kind of contemplation is not just a nostalgic reconstruction of something that is past and gone. This meditative rumination can lead us "both to repeat in our own lives the redeeming experiences of Jesus' own existence and to participate personally in the paschal mystery."[5] This brings us to the subject of worship and private devotional practice as a response to the resurrection.

Worship and the Devotional Life

The practice of religion is certainly more than what we do in ritual acts and in our solitude, alone with the Alone. But it certainly includes these practices. How difficult it is for us human beings to accept multiple causes for things, to think in terms of "both/and" rather than "either/or." A widespread interest in the inner life of the spirit has recently swept over the Western world. Many people deeply involved in social action have discovered that unless they have a vital spiritual life, they are subject to disillusionment and burnout. Without fellowship and empowering by a loving, saving God, their own love gives out.

There are two different aspects of our inward turning: our corporate worship and our prayer life, what we do together and what we do alone. Christianity is both a social religion and a private and personal one. Jesus of Nazareth took part in the synagogue and temple services of his people. He also went off into the hills to have fellowship alone with God. In a sense no one is truly human who has not been nurtured in a human community. We *learn* a language from our parents or from the social group. Without language we are only clever animals. At the same time none of us is fully human unless we can stand alone by ourselves. Until we can enter into our aloneness and separateness with peace and joy, we are still children clinging to someone's apron strings. We die alone, and there is a privateness in our deepest relation to the resurrected Lord that we only share with others who have experienced that kind of intimacy with God. Each of these aspects of prayer contributes to the other. Our corporate worship is enriched by our private devotional life, and our inner time with Christ is strengthened and directed by the wisdom and worship of the historical Church.

As my prayer and meditation have become more important to me, I have also found that corporate worship becomes more and more significant. Something happens when like-minded people gather together to listen to Scripture, to admit their failings, to ask forgiveness, to seek God's guidance and help, to praise God for his incredible love and power and to commune with the saving One. This sharing can be accomplished through Quaker silence, Methodist singing or symbolic action.

The Eucharist has been and remains *the central service of Christianity*. It was given by Jesus and was the focal point of Christian community and worship during those glorious years when the Church was most alive. Most of the Christians who were thrown into the arena were apprehended worshiping at Eucharist. They knew the risks they were taking and still they continued to come. In the Eucharist they met their risen Lord, and this was worth risking their lives for.

Eucharist provides a model for all Christian prayer; it is complete prayer. It contains all the elements I outlined above. Eucharist is a unique combination of praise for the love of God so clearly pictured in Jesus' death and resurrection and in the giving of the Holy Spirit, adoration of this love, contrition and confession before Love, absolution from God, listening and learning through Scripture, intercession, fellowship through the passing of the peace, communion and blessing. Many of the churches of the Reformation reacted against the superstitions surrounding Eucharist during the late Middle Ages and so devalued it. For many Protestant churches Eucharist is no longer the central act of Christian worship even though the great reformers, Calvin and Luther, both practiced and advocated the *daily* celebration of Eucharist. Eucharist can be the central means of sustenance and growth for certain types of people and needs to be available on a daily basis for them. For many people the symbolic drama of the death and resurrection of Jesus contained in the Eucharist is the royal road to spiritual and religious development. All of us can find this service a source of insight and communion. My wife and I have found that daily celebration of Eucharist is one foundation point of our Christian practice. In the near future I plan to write on the centrality of this service in Christian life.

The Inner Journey

Many Christians have forgotten how to pray by themselves. Few seminaries give any instructions on the practice of prayer, meditation and spiritual growth. What ministers do not know, they cannot pass on. There is probably no greater hunger in the Church today than for spiritual guidance and instruction in the art of prayer. One reason the Church fails to teach us how to pray is the pervasive assumption of our society that only the material world is real. Of course if that is true, then the inner communion with God is just wishful thinking or illusion. When at last we recover from the materialistic brainwashing nearly all of us have received, we can begin to appreciate the prayer practice of the early Church, the spirituality of the medieval Church and the devotional practices of the saints throughout the ages.

The early Church survived and conquered through the conviction that they met the victorious Christ and communicated with him in the celebration of Eucharist and in their times of private, silent prayer. The living, resurrected Jesus was a present reality to them.

Throughout the Middle Ages the monastic communities used the daily offices as well as daily Eucharist. These offices were settings for reading the Bible, meditating on its meaning and then coming to contemplative communion with the Christ revealed in them. This practice, systematized and developed through the genius of Ignatius Loyola, relies heavily upon the use of images in communing with the God revealed as incarnate in Jesus of Nazareth.

Another method of prayer that does not rely upon images is found in many Eastern religions and is popular in many Christian circles today.[6] This method is known by many different names: centering prayer, apophatic prayer, imageless prayer, the prayer of silence. Sometimes the word contemplation is used to describe this kind of prayer. Indeed in many circles it was believed that one did not come to the highest form of prayer until one passed beyond images into the dazzling darkness, the void, the cloud of unknowing. Prayer was a matter of detachment and passivity, of quietly resting in the divine presence. Basil Pennington, Kenneth Leach and Tilden Edwards provide excellent descriptions of the process by which we come to utter quiet, remove all barriers and rest in God. Our Western world is much devoted to content and doing, and this approach to prayer is an excellent corrective to our driving egotism. In nearly all genuine prayer an element of quiet passivity will be found. These two aspects of prayer are like the two poles of a magnet, both part of the same reality, neither able to exist on its own without the reality of the other. Contemplation can be either a quiet resting in the imageless presence, a personal communion with the risen Lord or the experience of saving love in the sacrament of Holy Communion.

It is hard for Westerners to be quiet. For most of us few practices are more important than learning to be quiet. To be quiet it is usually necessary to stop outer activity, to still our inner turbulence, to cease from our almost ceaseless inner talking to ourselves. We need then to relax, for tension is usually congealed action, being ready to pounce. Sometimes I find that fixing attention on a point of light, a phrase like the Jesus Prayer or the Hail Mary may help me to center my attention, or simply using the word Jesus. Herbert Benson in his book *The Relaxation Response* suggests the use of the word "one." At the point of utter quietness images usually begin to appear before the inner vision. It is like consciously observing the panorama of one's dream life. At this point one can bypass these images and enter further and further into the silence *or* one can follow the images and enter through the images into the subliminal state from which the images arise. In either case we need fellowship, guidance and direction as we follow these paths. We can become too detached from life or we may go on a dangerous way. We can become inflated at our spiritual intuitions or we can follow the wrong inner guide. The inner world is very real and contains deceiving entities as well as the saving, risen Christ.

I learned about the practice of inner life not in the Christian Church, but from Jungian psychologists who knew the reality of the spiritual world and guided me toward inner wholeness. Then I discovered that the same kind of practice had been used in the early Church and had been systematized by Ignatius Loyola in *The Spiritual Exercises.* I found three particular methods helpful in guiding me out of darkness, confusion and chaos.

I had learned that I could dialogue with the inner figures presented by dreams and imagination. And in the encounter with them, they often revealed their meaning. In a period of real distress I could not sleep. My friend and analyst, Max Zeller, suggested that the reason that I could not sleep was that God wanted to talk to me. Getting up in the silence of the following night I discovered as I spoke out to God that a loving presence was waiting for me and seeking my fellowship, eager to help me out of the

darkness and on toward integration and wholeness. Once I became comfortable in this nightly fellowship, I then found that I
could turn inward in this way whenever I was quiet. I learned
that the risen Jesus continued to stand outside the door of my
soul knocking and waiting with eternal patience. When I am
quiet I can open the door and have fellowship with this saving
Other. Out of these daily encounters have come much of my
growth, most of my ideas for writing, many insights about the inner journey and new understanding of the Bible. It is vitally important to realize that everything that comes in this way must be
filtered through the rational mind and checked against the wisdom of the Church or with one's spiritual guide.

Even before I considered the possibility that God wanted
communion and fellowship with me, I discovered that God
speaks to me in the primordial images of the dream. Human
beings have long realized that dreams speak significantly about
the depth of the human psyche, but it is not as well known that
they also afford access to the realm of the spirit. In the passive
state of sleep we are open just as in the silence of meditation, and
God speaks in pictures, stories and sometimes directly in our
own language.

Few people realize how much they dream unless they keep a
journal in which dreams are recorded. We can bring the dreams
that make little sense to us into the silence before the Spirit. As
Joseph notes in Genesis, the God who gives the dream can interpret the dream. What a sense of the providence of God is given us
when we realize that even before we think of turning toward the
Holy One, his Spirit is trying to correct, guide and save us
through messages given in the universal language of symbols.[7]

Another kind of meditative practice has been crucial to me.
In periods of darkness and depression the dark voices within
scream about my faults and follies, telling me that I am valueless
and would do humanity a service if I would remove my wretched
being from the face of the earth. Only as I became quiet and recorded these voices and allowed this mood of hopelessness and
depression to be translated into images did I have a chance of cop-
ing with it. We cannot change what we do not face. When I realize I cannot defeat these dark powers by my own strength, I call
upon the risen Christ to come and defeat the darkness within me

that has already been defeated on Golgotha. Inevitably as I call out for help with persistence, his saving presence appears. The darkness retreats in utter defeat and I am given a sense of worth and value by the source of all value. This kind of praying takes time and courage. When I engage in this kind of prayer I am allowing the victory of Jesus' resurrection to be effective in my life and I know the reality of the atonement. The darkness and the depression lift and I can take up my life again.

There is a great difference between *thinking* about God and *encountering* the risen One in these three ways of meditative contemplation I have just described. All three of these ways are more effective if we keep a record in a religious journal of our experiences of God's presence, loving and deliverance. They become more an integral part of us when we record them. If God really speaks and seeks our companionship, are we valuing this experience as it deserves if we do not record what is given us?[8] There are many different ways we can express our experiences of God's loving, saving, unfailing presence. We can sing or make music; we can record insights we get from the Bible or our understanding of how things fit together. How important it is to make a record of these gifts that God gives us when we open the door of our inner being to the One who seeks us far more than we seek God.

If indeed God is loving, near and available, how we deprive, cheat and short-change ourselves when we do not listen to the knocking at the soul's doorway and unlock and open the door and let the risen Jesus enter. The Holy One can give us so much love, understanding, and hope, such release from oppression, such victory and joy.

Love

At the core and center of Jesus' message and of his life and death-resurrection is love divine, all loves excelling. "Jesus became what we are in order that we might become what he is." Jesus loved us human beings enough to die for us because he expressed God's unfathomable love for us. We are called to live out love in our daily circumstances as he did in his. In the parable of the last judgment the righteous sheep are separated from the goats on the basis of whether or not they ministered to the hungry, the lonely, the homeless, those in prison. In John's Gospel, after Jesus washed his disciples' feet he gave them a new commandment: "Love one another as I have loved you." Love is transitive. It is not just my feeling of caring toward another; rather, love is the caring concern and love another person experiences through my presence and actions. The resurrection of Jesus has not become fully effective and transforming in my life until those around me experience love through me. One essential part of my response to resurrection is shaping my life according to the pattern of Jesus' unconditional love for me. This kind of love is not instinctual; it must be learned and takes unending patience and hard work.

Love means many things. It means social action, reaching out to the homeless, the broken, the discouraged, the confused, the poor, the suffering, the sick, the alcoholic, the mentally ill, the depressed, the hungry, those in prison, those addicted to drugs, and all who are suffering and are heavy-laden. At a recent conference Howard Rice spoke eloquently on the essential relationship of spirituality and caring for the many needs of others. He went on to add that our social action takes many different directions; it may be trying to offer people a new world view so that they are not automatically cut off from an experience of God's love. Genuine social action seeks to release people from limitations, oppression and suffering. Each of us has our specific role and destiny to play in ministering to human misery. If we try to take on all the problems of the world we usually bog down and accomplish nothing. Each of us needs to ask: What is my task?

Love needs to be a way of life expressing itself on many different levels. We need to love ourselves as Jesus loves us; if we don't we may be unable to love others like ourselves. Nothing is more difficult for us humans to believe, nothing takes more prayer than to believe that God loves us unconditionally. Next we need to communicate that love to those closest to us. If we see only the suffering poor out in the world and do not love those hungry for love and attention within our own families, we are in danger of hypocrisy. We then need to see that our casual acquaintances, the people in the office or the club, need our love as well. Does our kindness and concern extend to the stupid clerk in the store, the one who cleans the room in the hotel, the discourteous bus driver? Are we aware of the stranger in our midst in the subway, at the cocktail party, at the swimming pool? Do we reach out to them in a gesture of friendship and concern? Do we recognize the enemy, the one who can't stand us or the one who has wronged us or the one who makes our hair bristle?

Love grows as we try to love the enemy. God in his infinite concern for our growth will provide a new enemy when we have come to love the last one! We can also show love by allowing others to help us when we have need, accepting love graciously without constantly looking for the other's angle in giving caring. A personal journal can be an indispensable aid in giving us the opportunity to reflect on how we are loving and how we are failing and on how to plan our lives so that they may better express love. Growth in loving is a never-ending process.[9]

Another way of loving is sharing the saving, transforming power of the ever-present risen Jesus and his Spirit. This is a delicate matter. We need to be sensitive to where people are. Badgering people before we have listened to them is not love. Truly loving requires being open to others and listening. Then as they spill out their lostness, darkness, fear and confusion we can offer them what we have been given by the resurrected Christ. Not to speak when there is need is as unloving as speaking before we have listened. We are called to minister, not to badger and invade the lives of others.

These reflections are written during several months living in Malaysia where many different religious and racial groups live side by side; it is a country where Christianity has made little impact. The overwhelming majority of the people are Chinese with little clear religious foundation, Indian Hindus, or Malay devotees of Islam. I have talked with quite a few, many of them kind and generous people, but the ideal of loving concern as the core and center of life is foreign to nearly all of them. Christian and so-called Christian nations have not expressed loving concern for others in any marked way; however the ideal of love is at least present as a goal. Where such an ideal is not present it cannot be realized. One reason that the early Church made such an impact on the Roman Empire was that the pagans looked at the Christians and said: "Look how they love one another." They hungered for that love and were drawn to the Christian fellowship in spite of the risks involved. One reason so few non-Christians are touched by the resurrection is that they have not witnessed in most Christians they have encountered the love that was expressed in the resurrection.

One Easter at the University of Notre Dame I received a letter that I have kept for ten years in my desk drawer. It is signed "Mike" and I do not remember which Mike wrote it. After thanking me for my interest in him, he wrote: "I never will forget your witness one class day before Easter. We were holding the class in your living room. (We met informally there, sitting on the floor.) You were on the floor with a can of beer in your hand; someone asked you what this season meant or some such thing and you responded: 'It's this day that makes the whole thing livable. Without it the whole thing would be just a sick joke, a sick, sick joke.' You know, I've seen and heard a lot of people just about dance in trying to relate what it means. I guess it was the utter casualness of it all that made the impact . . . that was just the way it was, no doubt about it. . . . That's stuck with me, Morton . . . and you know what? You're right!" A casual remark in a situation where this student felt concern for himself as person struck home.

Courage

Many thinkers in the last two centuries looked only at the outer shell of Christianity. They saw the Church in collusion with oppressive governments and overlords. Freud wrote that religion was a return to the childishness of fetal life within the womb. Marx said that religion was an opiate, given to the masses to keep them docile. Nietzsche saw Christianity as the slave mentality of a people who were afraid to take up their destiny as superpeople. However, those who know something of the inner perils of following the way of crucifixion-resurrection testify that it is anything but the way of cowards. Jung affirms the testimony of all the masters of the Christian way; real following of Jesus of Nazareth is an heroic undertaking and requires all the courage, integrity, discipline and dedication that we can muster.

I am awed as I look back at the courage of the early Chris-

tians. Against overwhelming odds they maintained their commitment to the resurrection of Jesus, convinced that his victory
promised them more than all the world could give. They stood
against ridicule, persecution from their former religious companions, persecution from the government, death from torture or
from the wild beasts in the arena. Times of persecution have
often inspired the Church to its greatest heroism, faithfulness
and love. On a recent trip to China I visited with leaders of the
Church who had continued faithful even when their churches
were taken from them and turned into storage depots for rice,
manure or cement. The clergy were sent into the factories, dis-
patched to the rice fields or assigned as guards in warehouses. Recently there has been much more religious freedom; many
churches are open again. My wife and I attended services in a
church only recently given back to the Christian leadership. It
had been refurbished and was filled with old and young. I had
the sense of being in a first or second century church during one
of the lulls in persecution. Reflecting on the courage of these
Christians I realized how soft and spineless the Christianity of so
many of us is in comparison.

During the Middle Ages the Christian Church attained a
place of power and authority. Life was difficult and uncertain,
and for many reasons the Church emphasized imitating the suffering of Jesus rather than living in the hope and joy of the resurrection. Suffering was perceived as a blessing that one should
not try to overcome. Wearing hair shirts, entertaining lice, suffering through sleepless nights and wearing girdles of chains
were seen as signs of holiness and virtue. The ministry of Jesus to
the sick, the suffering, the poor was forgotten or neglected.

Most of the masters of the religious way of all major religions
testify that this inner journey is indeed a perilous one and requires the dedication of a religious warrior. We do not need to
seek physical discomfort or rejection by the world or the Church
to follow the way of the cross. Indeed sitting on a pillar for
twenty years or flagellating oneself in one way or another may be
more a sign of masochism or mental derangement than holiness.
If we will look into the very depth of ourselves and honestly bear
our failures, our imperfections, our selfishness, our openness to

evil, our cruelty and our disorderly passions, *we don't need to make ourselves outwardly miserable.*

Just bearing what we are in the presence of resurrected Love takes all the fortitude we can summon. When we really see clearly the shape of our distorted psyches with their anger, fear, rebellion and despair, we do not need to push ourselves further into the slime. We need rather to come again and again to the fountain of love which flows from the resurrection of Jesus, from the empty tomb. The most difficult thing in the world for most of us is to realize and to accept that Jesus died and rose again for us because God loves us just as we are without one plea. Once we do realize this truth, our task is to live in that love and share it as best we can with those around us no matter how often we fail. How humbling this is. Recently I received a letter from a priest friend who struggled with intense personal problems and finally had begun to look into the core of his being. He could hardly believe the volcano of fear and anger that seethed within him and could hardly stand the pain of bearing it. It took all his courage to deal with what he discovered within himself. He needed no hair shirt.

When I started working on this book I found myself unable to write because the darkness attacked me and reminded me of all my folly, failure and sin. This dark voice mocked me, saying that a person such as I was unworthy to write on such a topic. Only as I stopped and turned inward and became aware of the presence of the resurrected Lord who led me out to drink at fountains of living water was I able to go on. Twice during the time I have been working on this manuscript the same darkness attacked and tried to immobilize me. The more open we are to the spiritual world, the more we are opened to attacks of darkness and evil. I once complained to a spiritual guide that the way seemed more difficult as I went further; the answer given to me was that now evil had real reason to impede and stop me. Reading the devastatingly honest journals of Thomas Merton is comforting as they reveal the darkness he encountered and bore. The goal, however, is not to glory in the attacks but through the victory on the cross to overcome them as quickly as possible and go about our business of following and serving the Master.

In one of the encounters with evil it was as if the darkness had infiltrated into every pore of my being. I felt like the man who said his name was legion because he was filled with so many demons. Just as Jesus freed that man from his tormenters, I was freed. I spent several hours outpicturing my situation in images; I asked for the presence of my risen Lord, and gradually I found myself cleansed and freed and finally could feel again the love of God from which the darkness had cut me off. On the second of these occasions I felt myself bound and chained to the stone wall of a foul dungeon. I called for help, as I knew that I could not free myself. First I heard only the dark voices of evil mockingly say: "You called for us?" They laughed at me and went on: "We have you this time. You will never get free. We have you chained in the deepest and most isolated pit of hell. You will stay here forever. There is no freedom here and no light can ever penetrate this hole. You are chained near where our Master is frozen in a cake of ice. We don't want to lose you. There is none to free you. It took you some time to realize that you were in our hands. There is none to deliver you. Here you are and here you will remain forever." I continued to call for help in spite of the abuse they heaped upon me. Before long I saw through the door a soft glow of light. My captors were terrified and shrank back. The light increased and they fled to avoid it. One of them tried to hide by slipping within me and continuing the condemnation, telling me that I cannot be freed from him/her because I am such a vile fraud, so depraved and distorting that nothing can help me. I continued to call out for help and the light increased. Out of the light emerged the form of the risen One whom I find when I open the door to his knock. As Peter's outer chains were struck from him, so my inner chains dropped and my Lord rebuked the destructive spirit within me and commanded it to go. Then I was truly free, and I was taken to a secret garden, restored, fed and cared for. Life began to move again. The sense of gratitude lingered vividly for many days.

Before I learned how to invoke the presence of the Lord of resurrection, these times of hopelessness, depression and darkness would linger on for weeks, months or even longer. I kept going only by sheer determination. I have learned that the moment the darkness attacks, it is time to turn humbly for help, admitting my inability to deal with the evil within or without. Within three or four hours of inviting the victorious, death-conquering Christ to enter the inner combat, I usually find myself free. My risen Lord does not want me to suffer needlessly. He died and rose again to defeat these powers of evil with which my encounter is one minor skirmish. These dark voices can be seductive, and a Church that glorifies suffering can impede us from seeking the help that is available. We have to set our faces against the darkness struggling with all our human strength and then ask for help.

Developing spiritual disciplines gives us a good base to work from in our encounters with evil. The practice of finding time daily for fellowship with the loving, dying, rising God gives us the strength to stand and the continuing awareness that there is one *who wants to come to our aid*. Discipline and courage usually go hand in hand. In a world that considers only outer things and their importance, it takes an inner courage to pursue the spiritual way. Likewise it takes courage to look at the world and the evil in the world and see how little the message of the resurrection is heeded and how much it is needed. As I look at the poverty, the selfishness and conflicts between individuals and between warring social groups, acts of sadistic meaningless violence, and nations seeking power and prestige through violence, I have to remind myself that my goal is to be faithful, not to be successful. It is easy in the face of all this to lose hope.

How much courage it takes to truly care and love, to give of ourselves expecting nothing in return. To love in this way requires a death and resurrection; such love is dying and rising again. How subtle are our desires to be loved. I went away to Malaysia for several months to get this writing done. I found that many of the people I had hoped would continue to reach out to me did not, and I needed to remind myself that my task is not so much to be loved as to love, as the prayer of St. Francis reminds me. This is dying and rising again.

We also need companionship on this inner way. Sometimes the best of us loses our courage and stumbles down the wrong path. A spiritual friend who has encountered the darkness and survived is almost a necessity at such times, a friend who has encountered the darkness and has been brought through by the divine conqueror. Suicide is an increasing disease in our meaningless world. One important cause of it is the unbearable attack of darkness when no warm human hand gives us courage. Some years ago a friend was going through a very difficult time. I wrote him a letter which he and others have found helpful.

> Comrade on the impossible way . . .
> There is no hope, and yet there is hope . . . I am not me but
>   another and yet I am me also!
> You know love through me not because I am love, but an
>   instrument of an incredible love . . .
> a love like Aslan . . . a strange self-giving thing . . .
> The only power which turns back the demons, restores the
>   dismembered bodies . . .
> I died this week, and so I am much more alive.
> I saw my body lying there, and just because of this I am
>   alive again . . .
> And this aliveness I send on to you, this gift of death, this
>   resurrection, renewal, hope, peace and rest.
> It strikes you in the liver and renews it . . .
> It gives you yet another heart . . . new veins and sinews.
> The valley of dry bones becomes an oasis of living men . . .
> Life is more real than death . . .
> something than nothing.
> You have been dismembered and you shall come back into
>   wholeness with power . . .
> a promise.
> It has already begun.
> It is real and coming.
> Even trying you can't avoid the life and hope which come to
>   you.

> It is as sure as the wind blowing from the ocean at
>   Coronado . . . as sure as heat in Phoenix in July . . .
> You are destined to recovery and transformation. It is your
>   lot.
> You can't stay dead. The greater lover has ordained it.
> He is there . . . I am his harbinger, the first robin of spring,
>   the first tender, reddish shoot . . .
> The long cold winter, the deadness of Persephone is coming
>   to a close.

Christ has risen, Apollo is transformed.
Death is eaten up in victory . . .
and we can see the death of death in death.
Dracula is doomed. What is worse he'll be redeemed and
    forgiven . . .
How unfair, unfair, unfair, unfair . . .
The last laborer receives as much as the first . . .
Damned unfair, but the way is beyond unfairness . . .
All things will be brought together in harmony,
within the love which moves the sun and all the other
    stars . . .

It is ordained. It will be so.
Look up and watch it come . . .[10]

Responding With Our Minds

If our response to the resurrection of Jesus is to be total, we need to respond with our minds as well as our emotions, our courage, our prayer and our faith. Jesus came, died and rose again not to take away our minds, but to fulfill them, to save our souls and to make sense of our lives. We human beings are a complex mixture of mind and emotion, body and soul, conscious and unconscious. Christianity is not a matter of blind faith or mindless adherence to authority. Christians who do not respond with their minds are not responding with all of themselves to the reality revealed in the resurrection. Because we are Christians is no reason we should cease using the gift of reason that God has given us. Indeed if we do not use our mind with its ability to analyze and compare, we are likely to fall into superstition, bigotry, inconsistency. I doubt if we can truly love or pray unless we think through our actions and see the implications of what we do.

For several centuries our Western world has sold out to the materialistic point of view in which not only the resurrection of Jesus but even the idea of a spiritual dimension of reality has been considered beneath contempt, not even worth consideration. This viewpoint rests on very bad thinking and ignores a whole realm of experience. Christian theology in recent generations has not been much help, because it basically also sold out to this materialistic world view. What we need is a way of thinking that allows for and integrates the continuing, transforming *experience* of the spiritual dimension of reality in general and the encounter with the risen Lord in particular. Such a possibility is easier in our time than it was in the nineteenth century. Scientists like Heisenberg and T. S. Kuhn have expressed the growing belief that science has a very partial knowledge of reality and very little certainty. Von Hügel, the great Roman Catholic modernist, laid the basis for a theology of experience. He studied the life of St. Catherine of Genoa in order to understand the depth and power of the Christian experience of the risen Jesus. C. G. Jung wrote a letter to me in which he stated that the spiritual dimension of reality was as much a reality, a fact, as the material dimension, but that we don't fully understand either of them. One of the reasons I like to spend time in Southeast Asia is that it brings me into contact with several civilizations that have not been brainwashed by Western materialism. The spiritual dimension is very much a reality to most people living there. If we are to be knowledgeable in any area, we need to study and think. If we would integrate the meaning of the resurrection into our lives, we need to do the same. If we would share the transforming power of the risen Christ with an unbelieving world, we need to understand the roots of its unbelief and offer a more complete and meaningful picture of reality than agnosticism or atheism can provide.[11]

We live in a more open age than our fathers and mothers. We live in a world hungry for meaning. We need not only to keep our experience of the risen Christ alive and vital, but to keep abreast of the times and be ready to use all legitimate means to bring this reality to ourselves and our suffering world. We need to live on tiptoe spiritually and intellectually and keep our eyes open. My friend Brother Toby McCarroll sent me a review of Pinchas Lopide's book *The Resurrection of Jesus: A Jewish Perspective*. The author reviews the data supporting the resurrection of Jesus which I have presented and concludes that the resurrection as a fact of history cannot be denied. However, he draws different conclusions from the fact of the resurrection than are drawn in these pages.[12]

A full response to the resurrection will engage our thinking as well as all other dimensions of our being. An effective communication of our experience of the risen Lord will require the use of the best of our thinking capacities. We use our minds to master physics or the law or even to learn to play a good game of bridge or golf; how much more important to use them in our religious practices, which can have a transforming effect upon us now as well as eternal consequences.

Resurrection as Process

In *The Varieties of Religious Experience* William James presents an impressive number of case histories of people whose lives have been turned around by an experience of the risen Christ. I have lectured all over the country. I often ask people to write of their religious experiences and the effect these encounters have had upon their lives. The range and power of these experiences in every part of our country is quite surprising. Many of these people had never before shared their experiences for fear of ridicule from the skeptical, materialistic society in which they live. People can ignore or forget these experiences, remember them in a nostalgic way, or integrate them into the total fabric of their lives. Responding to the resurrection of Jesus or to the presence of the risen Lord is a process, a growing, an integration, a moving toward wholeness.

Unfortunately many people who believe that the risen Christ can have an impact on our lives fail to see that we need to bring all parts of our inner being before the Christ and that integration takes time, effort, energy, courage and perseverance. Transformation in love doesn't happen in the twinkling of an eye. Coming into the fullness of the stature of the sons and daughters of God is a long-range process that most likely continues on into eternal life. The first step in growing in the Christian way is the realization that Jesus and his rising are the focal point of life. This experience can indeed be described as being born again. The birth may come suddenly or gradually and it can happen many times. When asked if I have been born again I like to reply: "Of course, but which time are you interested in?" These experiences of the Divine can either be ignored or made the pattern upon which our lives are sculptured.

Someone close to me once asserted: "Morton, I have many religious experiences. If I were to take them seriously I would be a very devout person, but because I know that the world is meaningless they can't have a real significance and so I ignore them." Many of us have religious experiences but for one reason or another we fail to take the direction these encounters suggest. We may be so encased in the material world that we have no place for these things. We may be so overwhelmed by the evil around us that we cannot realize that dying and rising love has conquered it. We may not wish to make the changes in our lives that the resurrection of Jesus will require of us. The story is told of the person who started on the religious way at the suggestion of a spiritual guide. Later they met again. The beginner had stopped all his religious practices. When asked why he had abandoned the way he replied: "I saw some light and I didn't like it." Following the way of resurrected Love is not always easy or pleasant. We sometimes have to change the basic pattern of our lives.

Some people say that they are not interested in the resurrection of Jesus because so many of the people who profess it are not better than pagans and sometimes not as good. We human beings are very complicated creatures. Our psyches consist of far more than a simple clear will. So often we don't know why we do the things we do. We have many different motives warring with each other. We have our conscious personality and layer after layer of ourselves of which we are unaware. Meister Eckhart wrote that we have thirty or forty hides covering the depth of our inner being, hides as thick and tough as elephant skins. We need to penetrate through these if we would bring all of ourselves into the transforming presence of the risen One.

We pass through many different stages of life as we grow from infancy to childhood, through adolescence to young adulthood, through adulthood to midlife crisis, through maturity and a golden age to old age and eternity. Few of us live through all of these stages completely.[13] Many of us still have a hurt child or a frightened adolescent lurking deep within our unconscious. We are contaminated with levels of darkness which we pick up merely because we are children of a broken and selfish society. It is no easy task to face all of this and to bring it into the transforming presence of the risen Jesus.

True maturity is a process, a voyage and not a harbor, a never-ending growth toward wholeness and integration in Christ. To believe in process as central to life does not necessitate accepting the cerebral philosophy of Whitehead whose thinking is the basis of process theology. This point of view sees *all* reality as process and leaves little place for resurrection, spiritual communion, or the ultimate reality of Love as the Other with whom we relate. Process simply means that we are growing, developing, changing, complex human beings, and it takes our best effort and patience to bring all of us to transformation through fellowship with the resurrected Jesus.

The Miracle

The real miracle of the rising of Jesus from the dead lies not in the fact that a dead body was raised from death and transformed into a radiant transcendence. The Creator who fashioned the infinite complexity and magnificence of the universe could certainly do that. The true miracle is what this resurrection reveals—the inhumanly loving God. In spite of the evil, ugliness and pain of the world, there at the center of reality abides the Divine Lover keeping watch above his own. In spite of our failures, our rejection of love, our destructiveness, our pettiness, our violence and ugliness, God loves us and continues to reach out to us. He came into our world, lived, died and rose again before we human beings even considered responding to God, simply to demonstrate that love for us, to manifest the truth that God is Love. The Divine Lover still is knocking, waiting at the doorway of our souls to give us the simultaneous fruition of life without bounds; this destiny is offered to us now in this world and continues on to fulfillment in the Kingom of God beyond this realm of time and space. This is the true miracle proclaimed by the resurrection.

10.

Epilogue
Resurrection: Radical Love and Justice

by Howard L. Rice

In the account of the resurrection in John's Gospel, the risen Lord appears to Peter and, in response to Peter's declaration of love, demands that Peter respond. The demand of the risen Lord is, "Feed my sheep." Central to the meaning of resurrection for all of us is the response which is demanded of us. As we encounter the risen Lord, we are called upon to act in concrete ways. Our acts of love and justice are essential to our encounter with the Lord.

The resurrection of the Lord is an experience in which each of us is set upon two paths: the inner and the outer. The inner path of encounter with the Lord provides the motivation for the struggle to be faithful to the Lord's demand of us to bear fruit. The outer path of discipleship requires that we be fed and nourished by our personal experience of the presence of the risen Lord. The intrinsic and inseparable connection between these two paths of discipleship is a necessary, though difficult, one to keep in balance.

Within the last hundred years, American Christianity has been deeply divided between those who have emphasized the inner journey and those who have chosen the path of outer discipleship. This tragic division among American Christians, and particularly among American Protestants, has led to the impoverishment of the witness of the Church. Both the inner and the outer paths have become fragmented and distorted.

On the one hand there have been the privatist pietists who have delighted in the presence of the Lord and have rejected the ugly world and all its troubles. They have used the inner journey with Christ as an escape from involvement with the world. They seek to be at peace with God, and prayer, for them, has been a way of being alone with the Lord, nurturing the soul, deepening faith and feeling the strength of a meaningful relationship for themselves. The only reason they have anything at all to do with the world is for the purpose of evangelism. Saving sinners from the nasty world has been the primary agenda. This privatized religion has been highly anti-incarnational at the same time that it has insisted upon a very "high" Christology. It has rejected human values in the name of the Christ who was fully human.

Spiritual Christianity has often meant a rejection of certain kinds of sins, almost always the sins of poor people. The sins that cause the greatest fear are those which other people commit. The Scriptures are read very selectively in order to concentrate upon the texts which pronounce judgment upon divorce, adultery and homosexuality but ignore the texts that denounce lending money for interest, greed, gluttony, national pride or war. Privatized religion is always most concerned with private sins—with those things people do in bed, for example. Those sins which have great impact upon other people are of far less concern. Such an attitude is personified by the television preacher who denounces abortion as "anti-life" but demands support for the arms race as protection against demonic Russia and insists upon the return of capital punishment as the Lord's vengeance upon the wicked.

On the other side of the chasm are those who have rejected the path of pietism. Because they have been horrified by the misuse of prayer by those who seek only their own gratification, they have come to reject prayer altogether. They have chosen a path of discipleship in the world, seeking to live out their faith in their actions. In the name of their affirmation of human life, they have seen prayer as "other-worldly" and all forms of personal piety as a form of escape from the real world into which Christ sends us. They have rejected the inner path because of their deep compassion and sensitivity to human need. They have turned away from a profoundly anti-human, anti-physical, anti-sexual version of the gospel.

Dorothy Day, the founder of the Catholic Worker Movement, often expressed her horror at Christianity which ignored the plight of the poor. One day, as she was looking out at a line of protesting workers who were unemployed and without hope, she wrote these words: "These are Christ's poor. He was one of them. He was a man like other men, and He chose His friends amongst the ordinary workers. These men feel they have been betrayed by Christianity. Men are not Christian today. If they were, this sight would not be possible. Far dearer in the sight of God perhaps are these hungry ragged ones, than all those smug well-fed Christians who sit in their homes, cowering in fear of the Communist menace."[1] This compassionate protest represents the deeply disturbed response to nominal forms of Christian piety on the part of those who care passionately for the world for which Christ died and into which he rose.

The social activists have seen through the dangerous hypocrisy of much that has been proclaimed as Christian but is judgmental, harsh, uncaring, self-centered and individualistic. Their witness in the world of economic systems, racism, the exploitation of women and children, oppression of unjust governments, and the threat of war have been vital and essential aspects of Christianity. The witness of the activists has made a desperately needed correction to the flight of the pietists from the world.

The trap for the activists has been that in their rejection of individualistic piety, they have come to reject the nurturing strength of the tradition in the process. The early social gospel leaders were profoundly rooted in prayer. It was part of their strength and motivation, but they did not speak about it very much. Perhaps, because the pietists were speaking about prayer so much, the social gospel people were reticent about too much talk. Later disciples became less and less able to speak about their interior lives. They actually came to fear anything that might sound like religious experience. Their rejection led to a loss of touch with the source of strength for action in the world. Society is filled with "burned out" activists who have become cynical or despairing. They have often given up and adjusted to the world by becoming highly successful in the very enterprises they once attacked. Frequently they have abandoned the faith itself and function as secular people.

There are signs of healing today in American Protestantism. The so-called "evangelical" sector of Protestantism is in a process of revolution from within. The Declaration of Evangelical Social Concern, signed in Chicago in 1971, contained a ringing call upon evangelicals to attack American materialism and the unfair distribution of the world's wealth. The Sojourners Community has become an important voice for this new awakening within Evangelical Protestantism, and names such as Ronald Sider, John Howard Yoder and Jim Wallis are very significant. The social awakening of evangelicals has come from a recovery of the biblical roots of faith. It is also a recovery of the heritage of Evangelical Protestantism which once led in the abolition movement and the movement to institute child-labor protective legislation.

At the same time, Protestant liberal activists have moved to a recovery of the spiritual depth of their tradition. Discouragement with the high ideals of the social gospel which have not been realized is surely a major reason for this search for spiritual growth. Oppressive structures have been remarkably immune to the power of the trumpets of modern prophets. Jericho's walls have chipped away here and there and even cracked in places, but things continue much as always. What is more, the Church itself has been quite resistant to change. Churches have tolerated prophetic messages from the pulpit and have issued powerful statements at the national level, but the net effect of this upon the average church member in the pew has been either neutral or negative. The pew-sitter has either ignored the whole effort or has become angry and defensive.

The desperate need of the Church today in America is for a wedding of a deep personal piety with a passionate concern for the world. Piety without concern for justice gets reduced to a kind of sentimentalism. It becomes a path of the pursuit of experiences which become an end in themselves. The real goal of such piety is making people happier, better adjusted and more at peace within. Such religion becomes truly an opiate for the people. It numbs them to the pain and heartbreak of much of the world. It also turns them from their own inner pain. They cannot accept the darkness in themselves and they deny its existence.

On the other hand, a social activism which has no roots in personal piety can easily degenerate into a self-righteous pride which is filled with anger at those who will not see properly and agree with the proposed agenda. Such activism is very high on passing judgment but is almost totally unable to speak a healing word. Salvation, defined in terms of political freedom, economic redistribution and equality of opportunity for all, is almost totally dependent upon human effort. God's role in this work has been little more than interested bystander, giving encouragement, but essentially uninvolved. Great energy was required on the part of those who sought to change society and, as a consequence, many activists became bitter and were drained of their passion.

Kenneth Leech, in his book *The Social God*, makes vividly clear the inseparable character of politics and spirituality. He says, "The mystic tends to forget the one, the revolutionary forgets the other. If the solidarity of humanity is forgotten, mysticism becomes a form of spiritual self-delusion. But if the sacred value of each person is forgotten, if contemplation is despised as a non-productive luxury, if spiritual progress is seen as manifested in the world but not in me, the result will be a total disaster."[2]

It might be a cause for celebration if great numbers of people in our churches today were really serious about their personal piety or about their witness to justice. The reality is that, more often, the great majority is neither very fervent about prayer nor brave about social witness. Discomfort and fear of both activities produces a kind of dead goodness which is dutiful in the avoidance of flagrant personal immorality and strives for decency but has no passion, no sense of being grasped by the living Christ and no sense of complicity in the evil of the world. Churches are filled with essentially secular people who are not really expectant of any breaking in of the Holy Spirit. One of the potential strengths of evangelical Protestantism is that when people can be cracked from their narrow rigidity, they at least have a passion which can find expression in their concern for the world. A major problem facing most mainline Protestants is that they lack passion. They are comfortable, successful and without need for mystery in their lives.

Paul Verghese, a Syrian Orthodox Indian Christian, has identified five primary sources for the deviations of Western Christianity which have, in turn, led to and sustained the chasm between the pietist and the activist. In his book *The Freedom of Man*, he lists these as (1) a low view of the incarnation of Christ which neglects the full humanity of Christ, (2) an escape from the world into an anti-materialism which separates the sacred from the secular, (3) a low view of humanity which emphasizes the sinful character of humanity at the expense of the new life in Christ and, therefore, has little hope for anything which human beings can do, (4) an individualistic view of salvation which ignores the idea of covenant and pays little attention to the sins which are committed by groups or nations, and (5) a low view of the sacraments which leads toward the collapse of transcendence.[3]

All five of these departures from classical Christian faith are rooted in the same disease: that of fear of the material world and the separation of the material from the spiritual to the demeaning of both. A religion which holds the incarnation to be central to faith ought to be protected from such a separation. The incarnation proclaims that God is revealed in human flesh and that flesh is, therefore, the central manifestation of God with us. The incarnation is the basis for both true Christian piety and for passionate concern for justice in the world of the flesh. Because of Jesus Christ, humanity is inseparably linked with God. The apostle Paul expresses this connection, "If the Spirit of him who raised Jesus from the dead dwells in you, he who raised Christ Jesus from the dead will give life to your mortal bodies also through his Spirit which dwells in you."[4] Christian thinkers from Athanasius on have spoken about Christ being humanized so that humanity could be deified. Christ unites all human flesh to God in a new and special way. Thus the words of 1 John are central to Christian faith: "Every spirit which confesses that Jesus Christ has come in the flesh is of God."[5] Through participation in the living Christ, human beings are raised to the level of the divine. Human life becomes sacred. Such faith cannot separate the spiritual from the material, for it is precisely these two which are united in Christ. This union of flesh and spirit in Christ is the basis for taking all that is human with utmost seriousness. The world is touched by God because God saw fit to live here, to breathe its air, walk its byways, enjoy its sunsets, and pick its flowers. He enhances all human life because he was born of a woman, ate, slept, felt pain and sorrow and was touched by and loved other human beings. He wept at the grave of Lazarus, his dearest friend. To be human is to share in the nature of the God who was in Christ.

The union of material and spiritual is especially evident in the sacrament of Holy Communion. God in Christ becomes one with us in the act of eating and drinking. The sacrament can prevent us from making the artificial and unbiblical separation between the sacred and the physical. But even this means of God's grace can be abused into a privatized experience.

It is possible to have spiritual experiences which are not authentic. A warm heart is not enough. The presence of Christ must be carefully discerned. The Christ is always the One for others. His whole life was spent in service to the most undesirable people. He sought out the least acceptable, the most needy, the rejected. Any spiritual experience that does not lead us to share Christ's passion for others is misunderstood or imaginary. The real test of the validity of religious experience is what it does for the person who has the experience. If it leads to permanent withdrawal or disinterest in the world and other people, it is highly suspect. If, on the other hand, it leads to a radical love for others and a willingness to take risks on their behalf, then it has met the primary test for its authenticity. The opposite of spiritual is not worldly or fleshly, but lifeless, rigid, unenthusiastic or uncaring. Spiritual experience is the liberation of the human being from preoccupation only with one's self. Encounter with the risen and living Lord frees the person to care about others with abandon.

God is love, and the experience of divine love meets our basic need to be loved. All of us have this same basic need, and unless we are loved, we cannot love others. Unloved people cannot will themselves to love. The heart of the experience of God is the inner knowing that I am loved; loved beyond my deserving, beyond my comprehension, beyond my earning. This deep sense of knowing love shatters that otherwise inexhaustible need to be loved and the endless search for people to love us. The person who has been in the presence of the Divine Lover is filled to the brim and can go out to share that love. That is the reason why the truly great mystics of all time are such powerful persons. They are true revolutionaries because they have been freed from their own inner needs. They are empowered to challenge the forces of evil in the world because they know, from their own experience, that the power of self-centered evil within them has been broken by the power of God's freely offered love in Jesus' resurrection.

The Christian who has experienced the power of God's forgiving love does not have to deny evil or pretend to be better than other people. Spiritual experience, when properly discerned and authentic, does not lead to self-righteousness or to the dangerous effort to pretend that evil is foreign to one's nature and experience. Great harm has been done by people who try to deny their own evil. Such people seek to discover the cause for their own negative feelings in other people. They project evil on others who then become enemies to be hated or destroyed. When people cannot see the evil inside themselves, they blame others for whatever is wrong in their own lives.

Christian love is compassionate because it is able to recognize evil as a reality in the self as well as in the world. Christ never added to the pain of others by blaming them for their condition. He came to them in their suffering and need. To dwell in Christ is to share Christ's high regard for others. To know the power of Christ's forgiveness is to recognize that all of us share common weaknesses, temptations and failings. It is to see that all humanity is bound together in common need of healing and forgiveness. When a person has come to see that God's forgiving love does not depend upon one's personal decency or will power, then that person is set free to live honestly with others. It becomes impossible to rank oneself or compare oneself or exalt the self over others. The person who knows forgiveness knows how dark the inner shadow within the self really is. Such a person cannot judge others harshly. The power of forgiveness binds us all together in our common humanity.

Compassion is the heart of Christian love. To be compassionate is to identify with the struggles and pains of others. It is to share Christ's passion for others. Christian compassion is outgoing and active and is not content to simply feel sorry for others. Real compassion does something about human suffering; it cannot be separated from action. In his book *Compassion*, Matthew Fox says, "Biblical compassion resists the sentimentalizing of compassion. In biblical spirituality the works of mercy are *works*, and the word for compassion in the Bible is more often employed as a verb than as a noun or an adjective. Compassion is about doing and relieving the pain of others, not merely emoting about it."[6]

The separation of love from justice has produced a form of sentimentalized compassion which delights in feeling sorry for the poor and wretched of the earth. It is possible to get a good feeling from weeping over the plight of others. It becomes a self-indulgent form of narcissism. It is not enough to have the right feelings unless those feelings lead to action on behalf of others. To imitate Christ is to participate in the work which Christ does.

True compassion brings together love and justice so that caring for others demands a response to their need. This happens first in face-to-face relationships. It is never enough to love people in the abstract without loving the particular people whose lives intertwine with ours. Dorothy Day recognizes the danger of abstract love when she speaks about people who love causes or the workers or the poor but do not love individuals personally.[7]

Face-to-face compassion is a willingness to respond to the need for the person we see in front of us. Such love is acted out in the parable of the Good Samaritan. The more we care about the great issues which face our society and world, the greater the danger is that we fail to love the people around us. People can become means by which we can establish a noble purpose. This is a constant temptation of the activist. Personal, face-to-face love is willing to put aside great schemes and plans for the betterment of humanity at times in order to respond to the person next to us. Such love seeks to be caring, kind, attentive, and healing in all personal relationships. It is an essential mark of the Christian life.

The second form of compassionate love does not lead directly to other people. It does not satisfy our need for affirmation and the assurance that we are accomplishing anything. Such love is acted out in the way we deal with the structures of society. As we seek to transform these structures or re-create them in new and more humane ways, we are engaged in compassionate love. This second form of love leads to the arena of politics. It is as essential as immediate forms of love. It is impossible to love people as Christ loved them and ignore needs which simply cannot be addressed by our own private compassion for those whose lives we happen to touch.

One of the terrible tragedies of American life is the fact that we live in isolation from one another. The old are separated from the young in places of living so that it is possible for young people to go through years without ever actually meeting an old person. We isolate persons with disabilities in institutions where it is not necessary to see or touch them. We separate the poor in ghettos so that they become invisible. It is easily possible to avoid seeing the pain of most of the hurting people in our society. That is one reason why face to face compassion is not good enough. It ignores the terrible need of most of the people of the world whose lives are shattered by the cruelty of unjust structures, who suffer from war, who are deprived of basic dignity or who are without meaningful forms of employment. Long range love requires that we move beyond immediate matters to care about those we shall never see.

Long ago someone made this vividly clear, saying that if the Good Samaritan frequented the road to Jericho and if he found himself confronted again and again by people who had been beaten and robbed along that road and did nothing more than offer personal aid and comfort to the victims, he would be a fool at best. The Samaritan must begin to make some connection between the frequency of beatings and robberies along that road and some broader causes. Perhaps the cause of the trouble along the road is the lack of adequate police protection, or perhaps it is high unemployment in the surrounding area which drives people to criminal acts out of desperation. True love demands more than putting band-aids on the few victims we happen to encounter. Christ calls us to love those beyond our immediate touch. To feed Christ's sheep requires that we involve ourselves in political processes which make life-and-death differences for people most in need, most vulnerable to oppression or the greed of others.

There is no way to be responsible to the living Christ without becoming political. Doing justice is an important way of loving. Christ suffers with all who suffer, and we are to share in his passion for the "least," the most neglected and rejected of all. The meeting of human need to which we are called has to do with national priorities, economic systems, institutionalized greed, and military budgets. In our world, these are the powers which control the lives of people. The ways in which we respond to the difficult, painful, and often confusing issues which heal or afflict people are never completely obvious. What is required is that we act with wisdom, discernment, and, above all, a sense of concern for others. Effective witness in issues of justice requires that we bring together the inner and the outer paths. Prayer and meditation are closely related to the way in which we discern. Our relationship with Christ is that which, alone, can shatter our self-centered tendency to consider all issues from the perspective of how we shall benefit or be diminished.

The balance between the inner and outer paths of discipleship is essential but it is likely to be different for each of us. There are, however, some common patterns which may help us to model our own way of shaping the wholeness of our witness.

1. We can allow the experience of the risen Christ in our lives to motivate us to go out and engage in acts of risk-taking on behalf of others. Our own experience of the presence of Christ becomes the source for that involvement. As we are met by the overwhelming love of God, we are compelled to share that love in our own actions. Prayer and contemplation become the power which we need for our engagement with the world around us and beyond us. For many people, the relationship between the inner and outer paths is one of reinforcement and renewal. Prayer becomes the center out of which action arises. The action in which the disciple is engaged then, in turn, leads back to prayer. Discipleship which hurts with the suffering of others requires the renewal of prayer or it turns into bitterness and cynicism. A back-and-forth pattern becomes a normal way of renewing the self and then spending the self. Neither the inner nor the outer becomes an end in itself; rather they become ways which reinforce each other. The disciple who really cares about the world for which Christ died is driven to prayer. Prayer becomes a necessity in life, the sustenance for self-giving. At the same time, prayer is not a way of escape from the world but a way in which the disciple is empowered and renewed. Prayer also opens the disciple

to have the courage to stand against hostile powers and principalities on behalf of Christ's suffering ones.

The pattern of prayer and action may take many different forms. It may be daily or weekly. Some people who are heavily involved in lonely or dangerous forms of discipleship in the world find it absolutely necessary to take a day a month for personal retreat. Others establish a rhythm on a daily basis with times for prayer and silence interspersed with energized action. Each person is different and the demands to which each is called vary. Thus the pattern of retreat and forward movement will be unique for each person. The key is in the interrelationship between the two and the dependence of each upon the other.

2. A second form of connection between the inner and outer paths of discipleship is that of allowing the experience of Christ to alter our way of knowing and seeing. Christ enables us to pierce through the lies which otherwise hold us captive. Thomas Merton frequently spoke about prayer as the unmaking of illusion. To be in the presence of Christ is to know the world in a different way. Vision is deepened so that God's will becomes clearer and the evil of the world also becomes more self-evident. Prayer creates distance from the world as it is so that we gain new insight. This is a danger which all who seek the inner path must recognize. The more intense the relationship with Christ, the more clearly the disciple can see things as they really are. The blessing of Christ's presence carries with it the burden of knowing the pain of those who are bruised and beaten by the evil structures of society.

There is a sense in which people ought to count the cost of honest prayer. The answer to prayer may be a demand for something we would much rather avoid doing. If it is truly the Divine Lover who is encountered, we may be very uncomfortable. Idols of our own making have a way of making us feel comfortable and at ease with things as they are. The God of justice/love is the One who calls us out of complacency so that we share divine discontent with a world which worships death. We are met and challenged to live as people of the light in a world that loves the darkness. Dorothee Soelle, in her book *Death by Bread Alone*, speaks frankly about our fear of being disturbed. "We are afraid of the kind of experiences that challenge our sense of security. We are afraid to allow the petty bourgeois individual we were and are to be shaken and disturbed by such experiences. And that is precisely what religion does. We want to prevent religion from doing this."[8] This fear of what God may open our eyes to see may, in fact, lie behind our own resistance to God, our fear of prayer and silence.

We are so accustomed to apathetic response to violence, for example, that we can eat a meal in front of the television set while watching murder and feel nothing but amusement. Our numbness to the pain of others makes it possible for us to accumulate luxuries with little thought of those who starve for the essentials of life. Dorothee Soelle describes us all by saying that we are alienated from our true selves, "and our concern is to avoid pain and do whatever is necessary to put food on the table and make ends meet. Because we live by bread alone, we tolerate violence and perpetuate its structures. We give our allegiance to whatever seems to support this state of affairs. That's how we arrange our lives. We love anything that makes us unfeeling. We serve whatever regiments us and reduces us to just another number in the computer."[9]

To know the risen Christ is to know that life is triumphant over death. This knowledge, when it is more than intellectual assent, is the beginning of daring to take a stand for life. The Victor over death calls us to be instruments of life as those who share in the power of his resurrection. Spirituality enhances our sense of the sacredness of life. Communion with the Christ penetrates our own darkness so that we see the forces of death for what they are. We become people who cannot be content to be silent in the presence of death's powers. We become agents of life.

3. A third connection between prayer and action is the discovery that the risen Christ who calls us to enter the world of suffering and oppression is the One who goes with us. We are not alone in our struggle for justice/love. We act as those who work in the companionship of the risen One who goes with us into life's darkest places. Christ is encountered in the midst of pain, not in avoidance of it. Those who seek after Christ discover that they are met in the heart of darkness and suffering and evil. There is no way to have communion with Christ apart from the hurting

world. Once we have made this discovery, we are not afraid of being hurt. Death is swallowed up in victory, and life cannot be defeated by death's power. Fear of pain can destroy any witness. It can make cowards of all of us. The resurrection is our own experience as it enables us to discover the living Christ as real and present in the very places we would otherwise flee.

This personal conviction which rises from our own encounter with the risen Christ is what enables us to continue when hopelessness is all that our eyes can actually see. In 1791, John Wesley wrote to William Wilberforce to encourage him in his struggle against the slave trade: "Dear Sir, Unless the divine power has raised you up to be as *Athanasius contra mundum*, I see not how you can go through your glorious enterprise in opposing that execrable villany which is the scandal of religion, of England, and of human nature. Unless God has raised you up for this very thing, you will be worn out by the opposition of men and devils. But if God be for you, who can be against you? Are all of them together stronger than God? Oh, be not weary of well doing! Go on, in the name of God and in the power of his might, till even American slavery (the vilest that ever saw the sun) shall vanish away before it."[10] The conviction that we are in the company of the living Lord of life is that which can enable us to be sustained in the difficult, complex, discouraging struggles to which we are called.

4. To know the presence of Christ is to recognize Christ in the hurts of others, whatever they may be. As Christ suffers even now with the world's victims, we are able to acknowledge him and to share that suffering. This is the meaning of taking up our own cross and following. We can see the face of the Christ in the face of the peasant in Central America, the nameless, faceless slum dweller in an American city, or the Southeast Asian refugee. As Christ touches all of life in the power of his life, we are caught up in his overarching love for everything that lives.

We cannot be lifted to the heights of Christ without an aching awareness of the tragic condition of our world, and this knowledge is an essential component of any experience of Christ which is not clouded by our own self-interest or distorted by our social conditioning. Because we acknowledge that we ourselves are met by the living Christ in the midst of our own darkness, we can live with the confidence that God loves the most unlovable part of us. We can then meet the unlovable part of others without being condescending or self-righteous.

The recognition of the ultimate value of every human being is made particularly clear to those who are encountered by Christ. He illumines our minds to discover that we share joy and sorrow, hopes and dreams, pains and delights with everyone who lives. We are connected with each other, and this connection is made particularly evident in prayer and meditation. Henri Nouwen puts it this way, "In solitude we realize that nothing human is alien to us, that the roots of all conflict, war, injustice, cruelty, hatred, jealousy, and envy are deeply anchored in our own heart. In solitude our heart of stone can be turned into a heart of flesh, a rebellious heart into a contrite heart, and a closed heart into a heart that opens itself to all suffering people in a gesture of solidarity."[11]

People who claim to have had an experience of Christ which only makes them feel wonderful, full of goose bumps and happy, may be imagining a Christ of their own making. Christ forces us to deal honestly with ourselves and thus makes it possible for us to be honest in our dealings with others. As we see the face of the Christ reflected in the faces of suffering humanity, the warning and promise of Jesus that "I was hungry and you gave me no food, I was thirsty and you gave me no drink, I was a stranger and you did not welcome me, naked and you did not clothe me, sick and in prison and you did not visit me,"[12] becomes more than a metaphor; it becomes a kind of basic reality.

Encounter with the risen Christ is a basis for our own willingness to take every other human being seriously as sister or brother and to work for justice so that their humanity can be as full and complete as possible. Howard Thurman sees both the difficulty of doing this and the absolute necessity for it: "The willingness to be to another human being what is needed at the time the need is most urgent and most acutely felt—this is to participate in a precise act of redemption. This is to stand for one intimate moment *in loco dei* in the life of another—that is, to make available to another what has already been given us."[13]

The experience of Christ in his risen power does not lead to contentment, although there are certainly moments of great inner peace which are part of our experience. There is so much that passes for Christian piety which promises that all one needs to do is to draw upon the power of the Christ and everything will go as one desires. Genuine experience of Christ leads to a sharing of his radical love and sends us out changed, more aware of injustice, more open to experience the pain of others, and more prepared to stand for life and truth. No one has made this more clear than the great Quaker mystic Thomas Kelly: "The experience of an in-flooding, all-enfolding Love, which is at the center of Divine Presence, is of a Love which *embraces all creation*, not just our little petty selves. . . . There is a tendering of the soul, toward *every-thing* in creation, from the sparrow's fall to the slave under the lash. The hard-lined face of a money-bitten financier is as deeply touching to the *tendered* soul as are the burned-out eyes of a min-er's children, remote and unseen victims of his so-called success. There is a sense in which, in this terrible tenderness, we become one with God and bear in our quivering souls the sins and bur-dens, the benightedness and tragedy of the creatures of the whole world, and suffer in their suffering and die in their death."[14]

The union of compassion with spiritual depth, the inner and the outer paths, the love of God and the love of God's world, is a union which produces the saints who never choose one over the other. It joins each one of us with the great cloud of witnesses who have been met by Christ and who meet Christ in the neigh-bor, whether that neighbor is near at hand or far away and un-seen. It unites us with Catherine of Genoa in her reforming zeal to minister to the sick, with George Fox whose experience of God led him to champion the cause of emancipation of slavery, with Dorothy Day who identified with the poor by becoming one of them, with Howard Thurman whose spiritual vision enabled him to become the apostle of non-violence in a world of war.

When we begin to take seriously the presence of Christ, the fire of his divine love possesses us and enables us to love others even at cost to ourselves. Spiritual depth makes us enemies of the mammon-directed culture in which we live. We can no longer ac-cept its lies and its corruption, its callous disregard for people, its false idolatries of materialism, consumption, luxury, waste, war-fare and death. In the Epistle of James we read, "Friendship with the world is enmity with God."[15] In our own pilgrimages, the risen Christ causes us to discover that friendship with Christ is burning compassion for a broken world. We become agents of a radical love which sends us out with a passion for justice.

Conclusion

When all is said and done, when we have concluded our reflections, there is little more that we can say than the words of affirmation often used at Eucharist:

Lord, by your cross and resurrection,
you have set us free.
You are the Savior of the world.

Notes

Notes to the Introduction

1. Gerald O'Collins, S. J., *What Are They Saying About the Resurrection?* Ramsey, N.J., Paulist Press, 1978, p. 70.
2. *The Interpreter's Bible*, Vol. VII, p. 621.

Notes to Chapter 1, A Way of Hope

1. C. G. Jung, *Memories, Dreams, Reflections*, New York, Pantheon Books, 1963, p. 189.
2. In *The Other Side of Silence, Adventure Inward, Christo-Psychology* and *Companions on the Inner Way* I have described this method in some detail and given many examples of this process written by myself and others. I did not write these meditations for publication, but to bring myself out of the abyss and away from its edge.
3. M. Piers and G. Landau, *The Gift of Play*, New York, Walker and Co., 1980, p. 93.

Notes to Chapter 3, Incomplete Creation

1. In each of the chapters except the one on the resurrection of Jesus, I shall be providing only the setting for the central act of the drama of redemption and salvation. I have written a full discussion of the subject of evil in *Discernment: A Study in Ecstasy and Evil*.
2. I have described this process at length in *Myth, History and Faith: The Remythologizing of Christianity*.

195

3. The diagrams were drawn by C. W. Scott-Giles especially for the Sayers-Reynolds translation of *The Divine Comedy*. They are found in *The Comedy of Dante Alighieri, Cantica III, Paradise*, trans. by Dorothy L. Sayers and Barbara Reynolds, Baltimore, Penguin Books, Inc., 1962, fold-out at the end; *Cantica I, Hell, op. cit.* p. 70.

4. Victor White, O.P., *God and the Unconscious*, Cleveland, The World Publishing Co., 1961, pp. 192–193.

Notes for Chapter 4, Creation Continued

1. C. S. Lewis, *Miracles*, New York, Macmillan, 1947, pp. 146–147.

2. Raymond E. Brown, *The Birth of the Messiah*, Garden City, N.Y., Doubleday and Co., 1977, particularly pp. 25–38.

Notes to Chapter 5, God Present in the World

1. *The Collected Works of C. G. Jung*, Princeton, N.J., Princeton University Press, various dates, Vol. 6, p. 53.

2. In case one thinks that historians are truly impartial scientists it is helpful to read five or six serious historical accounts of some leading historical figure: Julius Caesar, Tiberius, Napoleon, Lincoln, Tamerlane, or Alexander. Sometimes one wonders in such reading if the same person is being described. Three books have been particularly helpful to me in assessing the historical life of Jesus: Andrew Greeley, *The Jesus Myth*, Garden City, Doubleday and Company, 1971; Gunther Bornkamm, *Jesus of Nazareth*, New York, Harper and Row, 1960; Raymond Brown, *The Birth of the Messiah*, to which we have already referred. All are excellent balanced studies of the historicity of Jesus.

3. Lev 11:7–8; Dt 14:8; Is 65:4.

4. Laurens Van der Post, *The Face Beside the Fire*, New York, William Morrow and Company, Inc., 1953, p. 268.

5. Kenneth E. Bailey, *The Cross and the Prodigal*, St. Louis and London, Concordia Publishing House, 1973. This book and *Through Peasant Eyes*, Grand Rapids, Michigan, W. B. Eerdmans Publishing Co. 1980, give a picture of semitic peasant life by one who lived in the Near East all his life and was chairman of the Near Eastern School of Theology in Beirut. He has written books in Arabic as well as English. His

insights illuminate many of Jesus' stories and parables and give new understandings of many of the New Testament passages. I draw heavily on his scholarship throughout this interpretation of Jesus' parable.

6. Walter Wink, *Transforming Bible Study*, Nashville, Tennessee, Abington, 1980. See particularly Appendix 2, pp. 159–62. Anyone wishing to penetrate the depth of the Bible meaning can learn much from Walter Wink and his method.

Notes for Chapter 6, Resurrection

1. Dorothy Sayers' book has been presented in many different editions. It is one of the most convincing and moving pictures of Jesus' life, death and resurrection. I would recommend it to everyone as devotional reading.

2. I have described the nature and variety of religious experience in Chapter 6 of *Companions on the Inner Way: The Art of Spiritual Guidance*. This chapter gives a background from which we can appreciate more fully the resurrection experiences given to Jesus' friends and followers.

3. Henri Bergson, *The Two Sources of Morality and Religion*, Garden City, N.Y., Doubleday and Company, 1935, p. 315.

4. In Chapters 5 and 6 in *Companions on the Inner Way*, "Atheism, Agnosticism and Spiritual Guidance" and "The Nature and Variety of Religious Experience," I have probed the problem of materialistic disbelief in depth and offered an alternative view of the universe. I have examined the problem from another point of view in Chapters 2 and 3 of *Prophetic Ministry*. The first part of *Encounter with God* summarizes the history of philosophy to show how we modern Western men and women fell into the intellectual bind of deterministic materialism. In my book *Afterlife* I also review the openness of recent scientific thought as a prelude to examining experiences of a non-material mode of existence. Unless this more open scientific attitude is introduced, the data of experience of the deceased would be denied out of hand. I have provided an annotated bibliography on these subjects in *The Christian and the Supernatural*, pp. 159–68. The finest summary of research in ESP is by Robert Jahn, Dean of Engineering at Princeton University, in an article, "The Persistent Paradox of Psychic Phenomena: An Engineering Perspective" in *Proceedings of the IEEE* (Institute of Electrical and Electronic Engineering), Vol. 70, No. 2, February 1982. One of the most perceptive statements about the need for a change of world view in dealing with human beings is the article of Roger Walsh, M.D., Ph.D.,

"The Consciousness Disciplines and the Behavioral Sciences: Questions of Comparison and Assessment," in the *American Journal of Psychiatry*, 137:6, June 1980. Both of these articles are fully footnoted.

5. *Science Digest*, July 1982, contains an article by John Gliedman, "Scientists in Search of the Soul," that brings the thinking of several leading theorists in science into review.

6. The full account of this experience is found on pp. 101–02 in my book *Afterlife*.

7. The full account of this letter is to be found in my book *Christo-Psychology*, pp. 123–24.

8. Dorothy Sayers, *The Man Born To Be King*, London, Victor Gollancz Ltd., 1949, pp. 316–17. It has appeared in several other editions. It will be noted that I have not described the scene of the setting of the watch over the tomb in my narrative of these events. This may well have happened, but it is the one event in the resurrection narrative for which the historical evidence is not strong. It is one that is not convincing to me, and I cannot write about it with the same conviction that I can about the rest of the details of this extraordinary event.

9. *The Interpreter's Bible*, Volume VIII, Nashville, Tenn., p. 418.

10. *The Comedy of Dante Alighieri, Cantica III, Paradise*, trans. by Dorothy Sayers and Barbara Reynolds, Baltimore, Penguin Books, Inc., 1962, p. 347.

11. This story is told by Arthur Gossip in his exposition of John's Gospel in *The Interpreter's Bible*, Vol. VIII, p. 793.

12. This dialogue has been taken from Dorothy Sayers, *op. cit.*, pp. 334–35. I have followed many of her suggestions in this scene. I repeat that her presentation of the resurrection narrative in *The Man Born To Be King* is the most convincing attempt that I have seen to bring together the various appearances.

13. John J. Brugaletta is professor of English at California State University, Fullerton, California. This poem, "The Beast in Bethany," was published in *Plains Poetry Journal*, July 1983, pp. 28–31 and is used with the permission of both the author and the journal.

14. This meeting is described in the last chapter of John's Gospel and was evidently added before the Gospel was circulated, but after the first twenty chapters had been completed. For those who wish a scholarly discussion of this story and the rest of the Fourth Gospel, there is none better than Raymond Brown's *Anchor Bible Commentary, The Gospel According to John XIII-XXI*, Garden City, Doubleday and Company, Inc., 1970. This work deals with the critical problems with good sense as well as with scholarship and interprets the religious dimensions of John's Gospel. I draw heavily upon this important work.

15. C. S. Lewis, *The Lion, the Witch and the Wardrobe*, Middlesex, England, Penguin Books, 1950, pp. 147–48.

Notes to Chapter 7, Ascension: Parting Without Sorrow

1. James Kirsch, *The Reluctant Prophet*, Los Angeles, Sherbourne Press, 1973, Chapter 13, pp. 132ff.
2. *The Hymnal of the Episcopal Church in the USA*, Greenwich, Conn., The Seabury Press, 1943, hymn no. 354.
3. *The Collected Works of C. G. Jung*, Princeton, N.J., Princeton University Press, 1978, Vol. 11, p. 464.

Notes to Chapter 8, A New Incarnation— The Coming of the Holy Spirit

1. I have described the history of this movement and the experience of tongue speaking which has often been associated with it in my book *Tongue Speaking: The History and Meaning of Charismatic Experience*, New York, Crossroad, 1981. I have provided in this book numerous examples of regeneration associated with an experience of the Holy Spirit.
2. Paul describes the gifts of the Holy Spirit in 1 Corinthians 12:6ff as nine in number. I have described them as belonging to five categories: the gift of healing and miracles, the gift of revelation in visions, dreams and communication, the gift of discerning spirits (the ability to distinguish good spiritual influences from evil), the gift of extrasensory knowing, and finally the gift of proclamation (prophecy, tongues and the interpretation of tongues). In addition there is the important gift of being able to love in the Christian sense and the gift of knowing and experiencing those who are a part of the communion of saints in heaven. Over the past twenty years I have written at least one book on each of these subjects as well as a book providing a theological framework making possible a belief in the action of the Holy Spirit. The interested reader is referred to the list of my writings in this book.
3. Raymond Brown provides a careful analysis of this passage in his commentary. In Appendix V: The Paraclete, in *The Gospel According to John XIII-XXI*, *op. cit.*, pp. 135–43, he also provides a study of the meaning of this word in John.
4. Morton Kelsey, *Tongue Speaking*, pp. 134–35.

RESURRECTION

Notes to Chapter 9, Response to Resurrection:
Release from Oppression

1. My book *Companions on the Inner Way: The Art of Spiritual Guidance* is my attempt to deal at length with the difficult subject of how we can be trained to assist others in their spiritual journey to full involvement in the Christian way. Most of my other books deal with different aspects of this response.

2. I have presented imaginative accounts of the crucifixion in *The Cross* and *The Age of Miracles*. I have shared meditations on other biblical stories in "Windows Inward," the concluding section of *The Other Side of Silence*.

3. Philadelphia, Fortress Press, 1970. I had not read Aulén's book until I had nearly finished writing this book, and I found the work of this impressive Swedish scholar supporting and confirming.

4. New York, Vintage Books, 1971, pp. 217 and 219.

5. *Theological Studies* 29 (1969), pp. 417–43. This method of Bible study is clearly summarized in his book *What Can We Say About the Resurrection?*—Gerald O'Collins, *op cit.*, pp. 104–05.

6. In my book *The Other Side of Silence: A Guide to Christian Meditation* I have provided a detailed explanation of the use of images in the theory and practice of Christian meditation. The practice of image prayer (known as kataphatic prayer) had been so little treated in recent years that I devoted the entire volume to it. In that book I gave little time or value to the other major type of prayer, imageless or apophatic prayer. In a more recent book, *Companions on the Inner Way: The Art of Spiritual Guidance* I present a more balanced point of view and describe many different ways in which we experience the divine.

7. In *God, Dreams and Revelation* I have shown how important the dream is in the Bible and among the Fathers and Doctors of the Church as well as in many schools of modern psychology. Indeed, the dream was considered one of the most important ways through which God communicated with human beings in some of the most vital periods of the Church's life. In *Dreams: A Way To Listen to God* I give suggestions for the religious interpretation of dreams.

8. In *Adventure Inward: Christian Growth through Personal Journal Writing* I have given specific and detailed guidelines for keeping a religious journal and many examples of these ways of praying written by different people.

9. In *Caring: How Can We Love One Another?* I have explored the centrality of love in far greater detail.

10. This is also found in *The Other Side of Silence*, pp. 282–83.

11. This is not the place to describe at length the nature of a Christian theology. In *Companions On the Inner Way: The Art of Spiritual Guidance*, Chapter 5, "Atheism, Agnosticism, and Spiritual Guidance," I have presented an answer to the disbelief of our time. I have also sketched out a theology of experience in my book *Encounter with God: A Theology of Experience*.

12. Minneapolis, Minn., Augsburg Publishing Company, 1983.

13. I have dealt at great length with these stages and their importance in *Discernment: A Study in Escstasy and Evil* and in *Companions on the Inner Way: The Art of Spiritual Guidance*.

Notes to Epilogue

1. Dorothy Day, *Meditations*, New York, Paulist Press, 1970, pp. 12–13.

2. Kenneth Leech, *The Social God*, London, The Sheldon Press, 1981, p. 29.

3. T. Paul Verghese, *The Freedom of Man*, Philadelphia, Westminster Press, 1972, pp. 55–56.

4. Rom 8:11.

5. I Jn 4:2.

6. Matthew Fox, *A Spirituality Named Compassion and the Healing of the Global Village, Humpty Dumpty and Us*, Minneapolis, Winston Press, Inc., 1979, p. 7.

7. Dorothy Day, *op. cit.*, p. 89.

8. Dorothee Soelle, *Death by Bread Alone*, Philadelphia, Fortress Press, 1978, p. 22.

9. *Ibid.*, p. 9.

10. *John and Charles Wesley*, edited by Frank Whaling, New York, Paulist Press, 1981, pp. 170–71.

11. Henri Nouwen, *The Way of the Heart*, New York, The Seabury Press, 1981, p. 34.

12. Mt 25:42–43.

13. Howard Thurman, *Disciplines of the Spirit*, New York, Harper and Row, 1963, p. 126.

14. Thomas R. Kelly, *A Testament of Devotion*, New York, Harper and Row, 1941, pp. 106–07.

15. Jas 4:4.